D1189542

Uncrowned Queens:
African American Women
Community Builders of Western New York

Volume I

Written and Edited by

Peggy Brooks-Bertram, Dr. PH, Ph.D.
Barbara Seals Nevergold, Ph.D.

Co-edited by
Lisa C. Francescone

From Peggy Bertram 2002

Foreword by
Dr. Patricia R. Fletcher, President
National Association of Colored Women's Clubs

Cover Art by Dennis A. Bertram
After a photograph by Rev. Willie B. Seals
of Emma Elizabeth Williams Ellis

Cover Design and Book Layout by Lisa C. Francescone

Address all inquires to:
Uncrowned Queens Publishing
984 Parkside Avenue
Buffalo, New York 14216

E-mail comments or questions to
uncrownedqueens@buffalo.com

Uncrowned Queens Publishing is a division of
The Uncrowned Queens Institute for Research and Education on Women, Inc.

Printed in Buffalo, New York by Petit Printing
ISBN: 0-9722977-0-7

Visit our Web site
Uncrowned Queens: African American Women
Community Builders of Western New York
http://wings.buffalo.edu/uncrownedqueens

To Clara Doretha Ellis Seals, whose unconditional love, unstinting support, and unselfish sacrifices for her children are constant reminders of how blessed I am to have this Uncrowned Queen as my mother.

To my mother, Margaret Gilliam Brooks, whose words I repeat daily as I raise the grandchildren she never knew. She is deeply missed, but the poetry of this Uncrowned Queen lingers on.

Table of Contents

Uncrowned Queens

Acknowledgements

The creation of this book, *Uncrowned Queens: African American Women Community Builders of Western New York*, has been a labor or love. We created the idea of the Uncrowned Queens Web site to celebrate the accomplishments of African American women in Western New York. Three years and more than four hundred women on the Web site, we are immensely proud at the outcome of this continuing effort to document the history of African American women and their contributions to the building of Western New York.

Despite numerous local and national awards and recognitions for the Uncrowned Queens Web site, no book of this magnitude could come to life without the continued support and well wishes of an entire community. The partnerships were as diverse as the women represented herein and include notable community organizations, church groups, businesses, and private individuals. Most notable of the partners is the Erie County Legislature through the efforts of Crystal D. Peoples; Buffalo State College; The Links, Incorporated; the Mary B. Talbert Civic and Cultural Club; Iota Phi Lambda Sorority; Alpha Kappa Alpha Sorority, Inc.; Juneteenth of Buffalo, Inc.; the Buffalo and Erie County Historical Society; the Buffalo Museum of Science; *The Buffalo Challenger*; the *Buffalo Criterion*; the Buffalo Board of Education; Humboldt Baptist Church; the Michigan Avenue Baptist Church; the Women's Pavilion Pan American 2001; Derek Byrd; and Brian S. Meyer.

We also acknowledge the partnership of the Uncrowned Queens Project with the State University of New York at Buffalo. The book project originated from the Uncrowned Queens Web site (*http://wings.buffalo.edu/uncrownedqueens*) that rests on the University at Buffalo's server. The project has received support from the Office of the Provost, the University at Buffalo Libraries, the Department of African American Studies, the Educational Opportunity Center, and the School of Library Sciences.

We applaud not only the Western New York community, but also our families as well, for assisting us on this very important journey.

Peggy Brooks-Bertram, Dr. P.H., Ph.D.
Barbara A. Seals Nevergold, Ph.D.

Foreword

As the President of the National Association of Colored Women's Clubs, it gives me great pleasure to acknowledge the work of the Uncrowned Queens Project. It has only been within the last twenty years that the study of African American women's history has gained prominence in historical circles. Beginning in the mid-1980s, amidst a burgeoning interest in African American women's history, researchers reconstructed their lives by excavating the products of their thought as represented in biography, diary, essays, poetry, plays, novels, serials, elegy, private correspondence, and other narratives. Uncrowned Queens: African American Women Community Builders of Western New York explores the thought, activities, and contributions to community building in yet another venue - the biographical sketch. It is particularly significant that the women in this book, many of whom might never have applauded their activities, were encouraged to write their own stories, celebrating themselves and their accomplishments. For some, too reticent to write about themselves, others wrote about them instead. Thus, the book provides a glimpse into the lives of Buffalo's African American community and exudes the feeling of multiple authorships. The brevity of the biographical sketch, compared to other narratives, seems to enhance the richness of the narratives as evident in women's activities in the church, school, sororities, community organizations, and their homes. They reveal a picture of sustained religious and organizational strength characterized throughout African American women's history.

Even a casual reading of these biographical sketches reveals their combined consciousness and activism as many women participated in the same organizations. Their commitment to their God and church is reflected in the vast programs they developed and supported, in both the church and the community. Through their individual achievements in professions from which they had been excluded historically, one can see their success at creating new images of themselves, gaining access to educational opportunities and career advancement, always mindful that their first obligation was to their community.

In the face of severe limits to their power, they found the strength to survive and to lift others as they climbed. Reading these sketches, one is reminded of Darlene Clark Hines' essay, *We Specialize in the Wholly Impossible: The Philanthropic Work of Black Women*. Accomplishing the impossible is evident in the "agency of their clubs or as the bedrock of the black church." These sketches reflect countless philanthropic endeavors of the few working to improve the lives of many. These women played a pivotal role in erecting the infrastructure of social welfare agencies, community institutions, political organizations and cultural programs. This book challenges historians to pay increased attention to regional studies of African American women so that these women do not fall between the cracks of American history and women's history.

The individual biographical sketch is the "mother lode" of the book, blending history and culture made available through an award-winning Web site: *http://wings.buffalo.edu/uncrownedqueens*. This extensive and still-growing Web site is testament to a century of Buffalo's history and culture in the black community.

Like other parts of the country, traditional accounts of a region's history and the history of individual states as well, has, in the main, ignored and excluded African American women. This book is a beginning in righting that wrong in Western New York. The marriage of the biographical sketch as a literary vehicle with Web-based technology, catapults these regional stories instantly beyond Buffalo and Western New York, introducing them to the world via the Internet. We have here an unabashed celebration of the strength and resourcefulness of Buffalo's African American women. As such, it is a contribution to African American women's regional studies; all the more significant because it grew out of an effort to remedy the historical oversight of the role of African American women at the Pan American Exposition of 1901. Further, it contributes in general to Africana Women's studies as it explores, through the biographical sketch, the contributions of African American women to their communities.

It is with great honor and pleasure that I add these comments to this unique and creative book. Three years in the making, and with little or no resources, it is an encouragement to the spirit of African American women. The authors have created light where there was darkness.

Dr. Patricia Fletcher
President
National Association of Colored Women's Clubs

Preface to the Book

We are indebted to the women who trusted us with their biographical information for this first volume featuring the Uncrowned Queens of Buffalo and Western New York. Family, friends, and the women themselves provided this information. A review of the activities of the one hundred women selected for this first volume reveals the unique diversity of the African American women who contributed to the building of their community, as well as to the entire region. Because we rejoice and celebrate this diversity, we refrained from providing a standardized template or format for the biographies, thus preserving the essence of this diversity.

Women from a myriad of educational, economic, and social backgrounds are represented because the struggle to survive and build a lasting community is not only joint, but a diverse effort as well. Thus, each had the same equal opportunity to be included. We will maintain the same policy of inclusion for each of the subsequent volumes.

About the Poem

The inspiration for the title *Uncrowned Queens* was derived from the poem, "America's Uncrowned Queens," written by Drusilla Dunjee Houston more than three quarters of a century ago. For more than four decades, Houston wrote voluminously across several genres including poetry, elegy, editorials, essays, and historical texts. She contributed enormously to building the African American community in Oklahoma where she was a giant among black clubwomen of her era. Regrettably, her achievements went unheralded and Houston became one of the toiling "uncrowned queens" about whom she wrote. In recognition of her achievements throughout her life, we dedicate this book in her memory and to her niece Laura Harris of Phoenix, Arizona.

America's Uncrowned Queens:
Dedicated to the Heroic, Toiling Black Woman
by Drusilla Dunjee Houston

The Black Dispatch, October 26, 1917
Courtesy of the Oklahoma Historical Society

'Neath a weary load upon dusky head,
Upon American streets is the tread
Of an uncrowned type of heroine,
Their labors untrumpeted and unseen.
It to her helpmate, life chance is denied
With undaunted courage, she stems the tide,
Meets some of homes needs, help make it fair;
That he may find a kingship there.

When manhood is shackled, into its place
Nature oft forces a courageous race
Of women, who with heroic spirit,
Stamp within unborn children the merit
Denied their fathers. For what man's disdain
Keeps from one generation, the next will gain.

We see them in rain, in cold and the heat,
As they pass us with patient, toil worn feet.
Behind some great universities wall
It is the boy or girl for whom she gives all
Sometimes the more sacrificial her fire
The less we praise it, the more we require.

Whipped with the lash, until the reddened stain,
Of her life blood ran from opening vein,
In slavery's hour, this type was true
To virtue. Today life's way they pursue
As heroically. No scorn or slight
Can change her ideals, she sees aright;
That duty done, in higher worlds will mean
That she will be more than an uncrowned queen.

Introduction

At the end of the 19th century, the City of Buffalo began making plans to host a major world's fair: the Pan American Exposition. The Exposition was billed as an event that would "fittingly illustrate the marvelous development of the Western Hemisphere during the nineteenth century...." [1] When the Pan American Exposition opened in May 1901 it immediately made Buffalo the destination for more than eight million visitors.[2] And indeed the visitors were treated to stunning exhibits of the latest in electrical engineering, medical, manufacturing, and technological advances as well as the literary and artistic accomplishments of that time.

The Midway, an extremely popular and financially lucrative attraction, was a major component of the Exposition. According to historians, most of the 8.1 million fairgoers made the Midway "a central destination" of their visit.[3] Covering nearly a mile of streets, the Midway featured some forty amusements, sideshow entertainment and "educational" exhibits."[4] In reality many of the "educational" exhibits featured people of color from various countries and cultures portrayed in typically stereotypic and demeaning fashion. Two Midway exhibits, *Darkest Africa* and the *Old Plantation* characterized people of African descent as either primitive savages or docile, but happy, slaves.

By the time of the Pan American Exposition, Buffalo was a bustling and burgeoning city with a population that numbered 352,287. The African American community accounted for 1,698 inhabitants.[5] Although small in number, this community had a history of civic and political activism. The "colored" citizens were equally as excited as their white counterparts about the prospects of hosting a World's Fair. As early as 1899, blacks had expressed to

---

[1] *Pan American Magazine*, 1899.
[2] Leary, Thomas and Elizabeth Sholes. *Images of America: Buffalo's Pan American Exposition.* Charleston, South Carolina: Arcadia Press, 1998.
[3] Ibid.
[4] *http://intoten.buffnet.net/bhw/panamex/midway.htm* Buffalo History Works. Reprinted from the Official Catalogue and Guidebook: The Midway to the Pan American Exposition, 1901.
[5] Loos, William, Ami M. Savigny and Robert M. Gurn. "The Forgotten 'Negro Exhibit': African American Involvement in Buffalo's Pan-American Exposition, 1901." Buffalo, New York: Buffalo and Erie County Public Library and Library Foundation, 2001.

Exposition officials their interest for involvement in the fair.[6] They saw it as an opportunity to educate visitors, both black and white, about the accomplishments and contributions of African American up until that time.

However, to their great dissatisfaction, blacks were excluded from leadership roles in Exposition management as well as in selection of the two Midway exhibits that were ultimately to be the only representations of African Americans planned for the fair. To their credit they did not accept the decision that these derogatory depictions would be the only examples of African people at the Exposition. In the forty years since Emancipation the Negro had made significant achievements and enormous contributions to the Western world. Buffalo's African American community was determined to showcase those advances.

Members of Buffalo's black community actively advocated for a voice in the early planning of the Pan American Exposition. Mary B. Talbert and other members of the Phyllis Wheatley Club of Colored Women were in the forefront of these protests and advocacy efforts. As a result, the women of the Phyllis Wheatley Club of Colored Women were instrumental in securing the Negro Exhibit for the Exposition. The Negro Exhibit was a display of the educational, literary, artistic, scientific, political and economic accomplishments of African Americans in the forty years following Emancipation. This exhibit, created for the United States Congress by Professor W.E.B. DuBois, Daniel Murray and others, had been shown at the Paris Exposition of 1900 where it was greeted with enthusiasm and received seventeen awards.[7] Following a protest rally staged by the Phyllis Wheatley Club of Colored Women in November 1900, Pan Am Exposition officials agreed to bring the Negro Exhibit to Buffalo.[8]

Rivaling the achievement of securing the Negro Exhibit was their display of dedication and sustained organizational prowess that left its mark on the Pan American Exposition. They organized housing and welcoming committees for colored visitors. They hosted socials and outings to the fairgrounds to visit the Negro Exhibit. As a

---

[6] *Pan American Magazine*, vol. 1, no. 7, p. 8.

[7] "Negro Exhibit at Exposition. Special Agent Calloway's mission, wants the Pan American to take the Paris Exhibit and enlarge it." *Buffalo Express*, December 24, 1900.

[8] "Contracts for More Buildings: Rhode Island commissioners report on the out-look for Pan Am and recommend a building." *Buffalo Courier*, November 13, 1900.

testament to their organizational skills and national prominence via the National Association of Colored Women's Clubs (NACW), they also brought hundreds of women and their economic contributions to the city when they invited the NACW to hold its Second Biennial Convention in Buffalo in July 1901.[9] They marshaled the support of their community in the wake of the McKinley assassination, initiating efforts to recognize James B. Parker's contribution as the black man who prevented an assassin from firing a third shot at President William McKinley. Legal authorities and the white press had discredited Parker's efforts.

Thus, one hundred years ago, black women used their individual and collective strength to challenge ignorance and racism. Through numerous efforts in many venues, they were instrumental in organizing and implementing activities that contributed to the betterment of life in their community. Their contributions are evident in secular and religious organizations, businesses, arts, fraternal and charitable groups, and educational institutions founded to support the African American community.

In the period since the Pan American Exposition, black women have maintained this tradition of self-help. Working tirelessly to contribute to their own community they often made advances and contributions to the community at large. Throughout this period we can identify black women who have been the "first" in their respective fields. In the broad landscape of community service, black women can be found in education, social work, health, criminal justice and law enforcement, the arts, business, religion and government/politics. Through advocacy, collaboration, and self-determination these women have been community builders. Often many have gone unrecognized or unheralded. Sadly, too many have been forgotten. The Uncrowned Queens Project was developed to address this oversight.

As groups in the City of Buffalo prepared to commemorate the centennial of the Pan American Exposition, the African American presence was in danger of being over-looked or relegated to misrepresentation once again. In 1999, co-founders Barbara Seals Nevergold, Ph.D., and Peggy Brooks-Bertram, Dr. P.H., Ph.D., conceived the Uncrowned Queens Project. The undertaking was

---

[9] "Bright Negro Women: interesting convention at women's union." *Buffalo Express*, July 8, 1901.

initially a focus group of the Women's Pavilion Pan Am 2001, Inc. The Project's name is derived from a poem by Drusilla Dunjee Houston entitled, "America's Uncrowned Queens." Written in 1917 to honor African American women, this poem conveys the essence of this project: acknowledging and recording the contributions and accomplishments of hundreds of unsung heroines.

In their roles as co-chairs of the Uncrowned Queens Project, Drs. Nevergold and Bertram consider this project a continuation of black women's efforts, of more than a century, to uplift their community. Further, they are committed to utilize this project as a vehicle that recognizes women for their unwavering service to the community and to document this history for posterity. The Uncrowned Queens Project has evolved as a dynamic program that has engaged an entire community and has traversed the world via the World Wide Web. Launched in February 2001, the Uncrowned Queens Web site (*http://wings.buffalo.edu/uncrownedqueens*) provides a repository for the biographical sketches and photos of more than four hundred African American women and recounts their achievements in the communities where they live. Most importantly, the project continues to grow.

This project has far exceeded the expectations of its founders. It has received tremendous documented support. After nearly two years of operation, the Web site has received more than 300,000 inquiries and usage is increasing steadily each month. It is no exaggeration that individuals from across the world from Argentina to Australia have visited the Web site. Hundreds more have attended Uncrowned Queens sponsored events. Women who are on the site often communicate personal anecdotes of positive experiences that have resulted from having a biographical sketch on the site. The quality of the site also has resulted in several national and international awards to date. Professional evaluators have commended Uncrowned Queens for its ease of navigation, originality, interesting content, professional design and unique presentation. Others cite the contribution of the project to the history of African American women in general.

Uncrowned Queens, however, is far more than a Web site. It is an educational project that utilizes the Web site and coordinated written materials to enhance the teaching of local history and indeed the national history of African American women. In addition to the biographical sketches, the Web site contains a history of African and

African American involvement at the Pan American Exposition of 1901. It also provides the history of black women's organizations, in addition to community events' listings and numerous interactive features that allow users to send feedback to site organizers. In February 2002, a monthly on-line newsletter was introduced to serve the many Uncrowned Queens subscribers with e-mail access.

The Uncrowned Queens Project continues to be an instrument to bring community groups together. Continuing partnerships and networks with non-profit organizations, community self-help groups, government agencies, businesses, educational institutions, and the media, demonstrate the tremendous potential of this project to garner widespread, diverse support. This networking has resulted in numerous community-wide Uncrowned Queens events, most notably the official launch of the site, in February 2001, and the first annual conference; *Lifting as They Climbed: A Century of Community Building 1901-2001*, held November 9-11, 2001.

Given the utility and diversity of the Web site, the widespread dissemination of information and education about the Project, the question may be posed, 'Why is this book necessary?' A goal of the Project is to provide educational materials to enhance the teaching of local history. This book is in keeping with that goal. Further, we have had numerous requests from the African American community to provide a "hard copy" of the "Queens" on the Web site. In response to these requests, we decided to publish a series of books that would be useful for individuals who are not yet computer literate, but who would like to have a book on the Uncrowned Queens for their private libraries.

This first volume contains the biographical sketches of one hundred women, all randomly selected. These women are grouped according to broad categories such as Education, Media, Health, Business, Community Activism, and so forth. Early in this project, we were amazed at the variety of interests and achievements of the Uncrowned Queens. This made it difficult to place individual women in the various categories. Therefore, we took the liberty of making assignments that reflected the broadest possible angle for individual women. Our goal was to focus the spotlight on those areas for which individual women were active, but for which they did not necessarily receive attention. Thus we hoped to illuminate our "queens" in very different lights. We hope we succeeded in that goal.

Uncrowned Queens in the Arts

Karima Amin

Native Buffalonian Karima Amin (nee Carol Ann Aiken) is a dedicated educator, educational consultant, published author, and full-time professional storyteller.

She was born on June 1, 1947, to Harvey and Bessie (Mabry) Aiken. She has two sisters, Elizabeth and Wendy Aiken, and three children, Abdur, Takiyah, and Sabriyah, who support and encourage her creativity.

Amin is a product of the Buffalo Public Schools (P.S. #75, P.S. #74, and Bennett Park School No. 32) and The State University of New York at Buffalo, where she earned a B.A. in English Secondary Education (1969) and a M.Ed. in Urban Education/Curriculum Development (1974). For twenty-four years, she taught in the Buffalo Public Schools, receiving numerous awards for service to public education including *Apple for the Teacher* (Iota Phi Lambda, 1994), *Teacher for Tomorrow* (Buffalo Board of Education, 1978), and *Black Educator of the Year* (Black Educators Association of Western New York, 1977). She resigned from the public school system in 1994 and transformed her avocation of storytelling into a vocation.

Her face is familiar in a community where she has been cited for several service honors, including an *Art Award* (Alpha Kappa Alpha Sorority, Inc., Xi Epsilon Omega, 2000), *Living Legend Award* (Metropolitan United Methodist Church, 2000), *Witness Our Women Award* (Langston Hughes Institute, 1998), *Outstanding Artist Service Award* (Alpha Kappa Alpha Sorority, Inc., Gamma Phi Omega, 1997), *Achievement Award* (National Association of Negro Business and Professional Women's Clubs, Inc., 1994), the *William Wells Brown Award* (Afro-American Historical Association of the Niagara Frontier, 1983), the *Daisy Lampkin Award* (The Links, Incorporated, 2001), and the *Community Leadership Award* (Niagara University College of Education, 2001).

Amin's voice is familiar, too. She has delivered thousands of storytelling performances, workshops, lecture demonstrations, keynotes, and libations for adults and children at a variety of venues. A long list of previous clients includes local radio and television stations, the Buffalo Philharmonic Orchestra, Albright-Knox Art Gallery, Toastmasters International, Artpark (Lewiston, New York), Strong Museum and Memorial Art Gallery (both Rochester, New York), the New York State Education Department (Albany, New York), the National Education Association and the Neighborhood Reinvestment Corporation (both in Washington, D.C.), the International Education Consortium (St. Louis, Missouri), and the African Canadian Heritage Association (Toronto, Canada), Chautauqua Institution (Chautauqua, New York). Her popular storytelling on a local radio station, WBLK-FM, has been a regular Monday morning feature for several years.

Amin's first published work of note, *Black Literature for High School Students*, was a textbook she co-authored in 1979 with Barbara Dodds Stanford for the National Council of Teachers of English (Urbana, Illinois). Her most recent major work is a 1999 children's book published by Dorling Kindersley of London, England called *The Adventures of Brer Rabbit and Friends*. In 1994, Galactic Multimedia (Buffalo, New York) produced *You Can Say That Again!*, an audiotape of Karima telling some of her favorite stories. Adonis Productions (Amherst, New York) featured Karima telling stories on an educational video, *Kwanzaa: An African American Celebration*. Her retellings of *Wiley and the Hairy Man* and *The Legend of Annie Christmas* appear in *African American Children's Stories: A Treasury of Tradition and Pride* (Publications International, Lincolnwood, Illinois, 2001), an anthology of stories, songs, and biographies.

She sits on the boards of Squeaky Wheel Media Arts Organization, Buffalo Quarters Historical Society, and E.P.I.C. (Every Person Influences Children). She is co-founder of several storytelling organizations which include Tradition Keepers: Black Storytellers of Western New York (1996), We All Storytellers (1987 with Sharon Holley), and Spin-A-Story Tellers of Western New York (1984). She also is a member of the National Storytelling Network, 50 Women With A Vision, and Just Buffalo Literary Center, Inc. (Writer-in-Education).

Amin has been invited to Goree, Senegal, West Africa, to share stories at the Family Reunion Project Arts Festival (December, 2002).

Karima Amin is well known for her heartfelt enthusiasm and conscientious approach to her work. Her biography appears in *Who's Who Among African Americans*.

Sharon Amos

An associate English professor of the University at Buffalo Educational Opportunity Center, Sharon Richardson Amos is the author of *Alabaster and Leopard Jasper*, a collection of poems and *Carolina Heat*, an unpublished memoir. She was born on October 17, 1951, in Lancaster, SC, to Henrietta Robinson and John C. Richardson. She attended Buffalo Public Schools (P.S. #74, P.S. #37, and East High School) and Canisius College (Bachelor of Arts in English Education, 1973). At the University at Buffalo, she earned a Master's degree in English Education (1986) and currently is pursuing a Doctoral degree in American Studies (Women Studies).

Her poetry has appeared in *Kikombe Cha Umoja* (1990), *Drumbeats* (1996), and the *Sunday Suitor* (1997); an article "You Again" appeared in *Mosaic* magazine (1998). Enjoying the opportunity to work with aspiring writers, she has served as editor of *The Wings of Imagination* (1995), a collection of work by St. John Christian Academy students; *We Can Fly* (1997) by Project Gift students; and *Poetic Lives* (2000), the publication of the ladies of Paradise House. Amos also is co-editor of *Telling Lives, Telling Loves* (1997), an anthology of work by Educational Opportunity Center students, faculty, and staff.

Always seeking to hone her writing skills through workshop participation, she is a former member of NIA Writers and a current member of Urban Arts. In addition, Sharon has engaged in workshops with David Henderson (poetry) and Masani Alexis DeVeaux (short story). Taking advantage of opportunities to network with other writers, she has attended the Detroit Black Writers Conference (Michigan), Moonstone Writers Conference (Pennsylvania), Furious Flower Writers Conference (Virginia), and the Sterling Brown Black Writers Conference (Pennsylvania).

Poetry readings have provided a means to share her work with a variety of audiences at Langston Hughes Institute; Theodore Roosevelt Mansion; Hallwalls; Central Branch of the Buffalo and Erie County Public Library; Allen Street Dance Studio; Gloria J. Parks Community Center; Martin Luther King Park; New Hope Baptist

Church; Catskill New York Reading Society; the Center of Inquiry; and Ujima Theater Company in the dance concert, *In My Feet is God's Thunder*.

Her community involvement includes membership in 50 Women with a Vision, the Board of St. John Christian Academy, Buffalo Genealogical Society of the African Diaspora (BGSAD), and the Afro-American Historical Association of the Niagara Frontier. She also is a member of the St. John Baptist Church and Alpha Kappa Alpha Sorority, Inc., Gamma Phi Omega Chapter. Her awards for exceptional service include the *Oxner-Lytle Award* (EOC, 1994), *Apple for the Teacher* (Iota Phi Lambda, 1996), *Torchbearer of Service* (SJBC, 1996), and the Bambara Lorde Fellowship (2000).

An avid reader, Sharon is one of the cofounders of Maumbusoma: Sisters Reading (1992). She also enjoys the poetry of Nikki Giovanni and Georgia Douglas Johnson.

She has one son, Jason Barrington Amos.

Agnes M. Bain

Agnes M. Bain is the Executive Director of the African American Cultural Center where she is responsible for the development and coordination of administrative and programmatic organizational policies. In her twenty-three years of administration, she has increased the Center's budget to include grants from the United Way of Buffalo and Erie County, the New York State Council on the Arts, the National Endowment for the Arts, the Office of Children and Family Services, the Western New York Congressional Delegation, the City of Buffalo, the County of Erie, the Erie County Department of Youth Services, the New York State Division for Youth Special Legislative Grant, the New York State Department of State, and various corporations. In the forty-two year history of the African American Cultural Center, Ms. Bain obtained the first grant to completely renovate the facility.

She has produced over eighty African American productions working with such notables as Woodie King, Jr. (New York City producer/director/writer), Phylicia Ayers-Allen (*Bill Cosby Show*), Richard Gant (*Rocky II*), Karen White (*Bill Cosby Show* and *Lean on Me*), Theresa Merritt (renowned Broadway actress), Bill Cobb (*The Bodyguard*), not to forget Buffalo's Edward Lawrence, Edward G. Smith, Lorna C. Hill, Timothy Kennedy, Laverne Clay, and Fortunato Pezzimenti. She has produced over twenty-eight jazz concerts with such notables as Jimmy McGriff, Bill Doggett, Billy Taylor, Horace Silver, Houston Pearson, Etta Jones, Milt Jackson, Johnny Lytle, Hank Crawford, and Gloria Lynn, just to name a few and not to exclude Buffalo's own Jaman, DoDo Green, James "Pappy" Martin, and Count Rabbit. She has worked with renowned dancers -- Pearl Primus, Mike Malone (Debbie Allen's teacher), Rod Rodgers, and Babatunde Olatunji. She presented plaques of distinction to Johnny Mathis, Cicely Tyson, and Ted Lange, welcoming them to Buffalo.

Ms. Bain has been a Board Member of the East Side Coalition of the Arts, Niagara Frontier Folk Art Council, and Tashama's Childrens' Repertoire Performance Workshop. She is a past member to Buffalo's Art Commission appointed by Mayor Anthony M. Masiello, and a former panel member to the New York State Council on the Arts/Special Arts Service Program. She is a Board member to the Arts Council of Buffalo and Erie County, and a panelist for the Decentralization and Key Bank Art Grants sponsored by the Arts Council of Buffalo and Erie County.

Ms. Bain has received many awards for leadership, dedication to the community and distinguished achievements. She received the Appreciation for Services award from Councilman David Collins and Al Styles of the Concerned Citizens Committee. Other awards include those from the Langston Hughes Institute; Kenfield/Langfield Association; Board of Directors, African American Cultural Center; Martin Luther King Committee; Lighthouse Inter-Denominational Ministries, Inc.; Cold Spring Block Club; Buffalo Club National Association of Negro Business and Professional Women's Clubs, Inc.; Black Achievers; Agape AME Church; Naomi Chapter No. 10 – Order of the Eastern Star Prince Hall Affiliation; and a State of New York Legislative Resolution presented by former State Senator Anthony Nanula.

Lois Josephine Barnes-Easley

Lois Josephine Barnes was born on September 17, 1909, in Olean, New York. Her parents are Oliver and Olive Cady Barnes. Miss Barnes married Robert Easley on February 4, 1928.

Following in the footsteps of her mother and grandmother, Mrs. Easley became an accomplished pianist at a very early age. She not only used her musical talent as a source of employment, she also gave freely to the community, playing benefit concerts for groups such as the Red Cross, March of Dimes, Gold Star Mothers, American Legion, the Olean Service Club, area veterans' hospitals, and other charitable and civic organizations.

She would accompany high school students at annual music competitions and attended many auditions with her daughter, Lois, and son, William, in addition to those of her grandsons, Reginal and Timothy Spiller. Many Olean High School students would request Mrs. Easley to accompany them when they auditioned for music colleges.

In the late 1950s, she was den mother for Cub Scout Troop 87, Den 5.

Mrs. Easley, and her husband, who was a drummer, played with the Bob Easley Band at clubs and dances throughout Olean, Western New York, and Pennsylvania from 1929 to the mid-1960s. For a brief period in the 1940s, she had her own band.

She was a pianist at Bethel AME Church after her mother was unable to continue as the church organist. She was honored by Bethel AME Church in 1991, for her forty years of volunteer service.

In addition to her musical talent, Mrs. Easley was a poet who wrote over one hundred unpublished poems since 1959. The Friends of the Olean Library honored her for her poetry in 1996. In 1997, Mrs. Easley, along with her son, William, received the first *Regina A. Quick Arts* award from St. Bonaventure University.

Mrs. Easley died in Olean on November 19, 2000, at the age of 92.

Patricia Carter

Patricia A. Carter began her art studies in 1979, while pursuing a Bachelor of Arts Degree at Cornell University. She earned a Masters Degree in Urban and Regional Planning from the University of California at Berkeley. In addition, she was an adjunct professor in the School of Landscape Architecture and Planning at Arizona State University.

She studied painting at the Luminous Workshop in Buffalo and monotype printmaking at Buffalo State College. Since 1993, she has participated in several juried shows in Western New York, including shows at the Albright-Knox Art Gallery, the Castellani Art Museum, Impact Women's Gallery, and Hallwalls Contemporary Art Museum. Patricia received an honorable mention award from Nancy Weekly and Charles Cary Rumsey the curator of the Burchfield-Penney Art Center, for one of two works exhibited at the Impact Gallery, *Covering/Uncovering* national exhibition in 1995. In June 1997, she had a solo exhibition of her work sponsored by El Museo Francisco Oller Y Diego Rivera Gallery.

Her artwork was published by the Poetry Collection at the University at Buffalo following a solo exhibit there in November 1997. In February 2000, she had a solo exhibition of her work at the Phoenix Downtown Magazine in Phoenix, Arizona.

Patricia teaches children in the *Art with Artists* program conducted by the Albright-Knox Art Gallery Education Department. She completed an Artist-in-Residence at the Edna Manley College of Visual Arts in Kingston, Jamaica, West Indies, in 1998.

She has been a member of the Board of Directors of Hallwalls Contemporary Art Center. Her work is included in the Burchfield-Penney Art Center's Museum Collection and various private art collections in the United States and Canada.

Alexis DeVeaux

Alexis DeVeaux is a poet, short fiction writer, essayist, educator, and biographer whose work is nationally and internationally known. Born and raised in Harlem, New York, Ms. DeVeaux has published in five languages: English, Spanish, Dutch, Japanese, and Serbo-Croatian.

Among her works are a fictionalized memoir, *Spirits: In The Street* (Doubleday, 1973); an award-winning children's book, *Na-Ni* (Harper and Row, 1973); *Don't Explain, a Biography of Jazz Great, Billie Holiday* (Harper and Row, 1980); two independently published poetry works, *Blue Beat: A Portfolio of Poems and Drawings* (1985) and *Spirit Talk* (1997); and a second children's book, *An Enchanted Hair Tale* (Harper and Row, 1987), which was a recipient of the 1988 *Coretta Scott King Award* presented by the American Library Association and the 1991 *Lorraine Hansberry Award for Excellence in Children's Literature.*

In 1997, one of her poems was selected for the prestigious Christmas Broadside Series published under the auspices of the Friends of the University Libraries, the State University of New York at Buffalo. Her plays have been produced on television, off-Broadway, and in regional theaters and include *Circles* (1972); *The Tapestry* (1976); *A Season to Unravel* (1979); *NO* (1981); and *Elbow Rooms* (1987).

A diversified writer, her poems, short stories, and articles have appeared in numerous anthologies and publications, including *Essence Magazine; The New York Village Voice; The Iowa Review; Home Girls, A Black Feminist Anthology; Emerge Magazine; The Utne Reader; Confirmation, An Anthology of African American Women; Midnight Birds, Stories by Contemporary Black Women Writers; Sage, A Scholarly Journal on Black Women; Children of the Night, The Best Short Stories by Black Writers, 1967 to the Present; Street Lights, Illuminating Tales of the Urban Black Experience; Afrekete, An Anthology of Black Lesbian Writing; Memory of Kin, Stories About Family by Black Writers; Circles, Buffalo Women's Journal of Law and Social Policy; Does Your Mama Know?, An Anthology of Black Lesbian Coming Out Stories; The Wild Good, Lesbian*

Photographs and Writing on Love; *Liberating Memory, Our Work and Working-class Consciousness*; and *Callaloo: A Journal of Afro-American and African Arts and Letters*. In other media, Ms. DeVeaux's work appears on several records including the highly acclaimed album, *Sisterfire* for Olivia Records. In 1986 she produced the independent video documentary, *MOTHERLANDS: From Manhattan to Manague to Africa, Hand in Hand*. This was done in association with the MADRE Video Project.

As an artist and lecturer, she has traveled extensively throughout the United States, the Caribbean, Africa, Japan, and Europe; and is recognized for her contributions to such organizations as MADRE, an international women's self-help organization; SISA (Sisterhood in Support of Sisters in South Africa); the Brooklyn-based performance collective, Flamboyant Ladies Theater Company (co-founded with actress Gwendolen Hardwick; 1979-1986); the Organization of Women Writers of Africa (OWWA); the Buffalo Quarters Historical Society; Just Buffalo Literary Center; the Arts Council of Buffalo and Erie County; and the Association of Caribbean Women Writers and Scholars (ACWWS). Over the years, Ms. DeVeaux has combined her interests in creativity, social change, and education; and has taught in community-based organizations, libraries and public schools as well as at several institutions, including Sarah Lawrence College (Bronxville, New York), Vermont College (Vermont), Wabash College (Indiana), and Erie Community College (Buffalo, New York). At present, she is a member of the faculty of the State University of New York at Buffalo where, as an Associate Professor, she teaches in the Department of Women's Studies. Ms. DeVeaux has a Ph.D. in American Studies and recently completed a biography of the late poet Audre Lorde.

Wilhelmina M. Godfrey

Born in Philadelphia, Pennsylvania, Wilhelmina McAlpin was raised and educated in Buffalo. She was married to William Godfrey, Jr., for fifty-eight years and they had one child, Carol Godfrey Wing.

She once told a reporter that she had drawn and painted all her life. She took all the art classes available at Fosdick Masten Park High School, but the Depression interrupted her art education until the mid-1940s, when she won scholarships to the Art Institute of Buffalo and the Albright Art School. Her paintings from that era documented life on Buffalo's east side. In 1951, she organized and taught painting and drawing classes at the former Michigan Avenue YMCA in Buffalo.

In 1958, she began weaving after seeing an exhibit in Rochester, New York and produced abstract works that borrowed themes and designs from African art.

She was an artist for eleven years at AM&A's department store, leaving in 1963 to pursue her studio work full time. She organized the weaving department at the University at Buffalo and was an instructor at its Creative Craft Center from 1967 to 1970. She also was a founder and director of the Langston Hughes Center. During this period, Wilhelmina organized and taught creative craft classes at St. Philip's Episcopal Church's Community Center.

In 1974, she received a craftsmen's fellowship from the National Endowment for the Arts and earned a scholarship to the Haystack Mountain School of Crafts in Deer Isle, Maine. She served as Crafts Adviser to the Buffalo Wider Horizons Craft Program, the National Endowment for the Arts craftsmen's fellowship in 1976. In 1979, she presented a paper with slides titled *The Negro Slave Crafts Workers of North and South Carolina* at the first National African American Crafts Conference Symposium in Memphis, Tennessee.

Her commissions included a triptych altar painting for St. Philip's Episcopal Church and a five-panel altar painting for St. Matthew's Episcopal Church in Buffalo. In 1990, she was recognized with the Buffalo and Erie County Arts Council's *Individual Artist Within the*

Community Award. During that same year, a retrospective of her paintings, prints, and weaving was exhibited at Medaille College, which created a gallery so it could display her works.

In December 1994, the Burchfield-Penney Art Center's Art Committee voted to accept Wilhelmina's *City Playground, 1949-50* for inclusion in the permanent collection. The work was donated by her husband and daughter. Mrs. Godfrey's works have been purchased locally and across the United States.

She was a life member of the Albright-Knox Art Gallery; past officer of the Albright-Knox Members Council and the Buffalo Craftsmen; board member of the New York State Craftsmen; member of the African American Crafts Council, the American Sector of the World Crafts Council; member of the National Conference of Artists; and member of Arts Development Services of Buffalo. She also was a member of the advisory board for the Arts Committee for Erie Community College City Campus and the art advisory committee of Buffalo's Metro Rail system.

Mrs. Godfrey was a seventy-year member of St. Philip's Episcopal Church. She organized the church's Girls Friendly Society in 1951, and was a past president of St. Philip's Episcopal Churchwomen. She also was a member of St. Philip's Community Center, past member of the Episcopal Diocese of Western New York's Church Mission of Help, and chairwoman of Episcopal Churchwomen for the Central Erie Deanery from 1968 to 1970.

She was a past president of Beta Phi Chapter of Iota Phi Lambda sorority and was the sorority's journalist for the Eastern Region and assistant to its national publicity chairman. Mrs. Godfrey was a gourmet cook, an avid fisherman, and a creative seamstress.

Mrs. Godfrey was a past member of the Democratic Business and Professional Women's Club of the Niagara Frontier, the Neighborhood House Association, and the National Association for the Advancement of Colored People.

Lorna C. Hill

In 1978, Lorna C. Hill became the Founder and Executive Director of the Ujima Theater Company, Inc., the oldest professional repertory theater company in Western New York. Ujima, a multicultural membership organization, is dedicated to providing a vehicle for African American performers, theater crafts people, and administrators.

Her experience as an actress includes stage, feature film, television, commercial, industrial film, and voice-over productions. Ms. Hill also is known as a storyteller par excellence. She is a playwright and poet who is best known for the play *Yalla Bitch* that was performed as part of the first International Women Playwrights Conference.

Lorna provides consultant services to agencies and serves as a guest speaker for organizations whose agendas include women's issues, arts and culture, children's rights, and ending racism. In addition, Ms. Hill is a teacher who provides writing workshops, acting lessons, interview techniques training, and in-service training to teachers in the use of culture as an academic resource.

She was the first African American woman accepted at Dartmouth College where she earned a Bachelor of Arts degree in American Intellectual History in 1973. In 1978, she earned a Master of Arts in Theater from the University at Buffalo where she is currently a Ph.D. Candidate.

Ms. Hill is a single mother of two children, Amilcar Cabral and Zoe Viola.

Celeste Lawson

Celeste Lawson has nearly twenty-five years of experience in non-profit management and arts administration. Currently, she is the Executive Director of the Arts Council of Buffalo and Erie County, an organization that provides a variety of services to artists and arts organizations throughout Erie County, with supporting programs in Niagara, Allegany, Chautauqua, and Cattaraugus counties. Prior to her appointment at the Arts Council, Ms. Lawson was Executive Director of the King Urban Life Center, a local historical preservation and adaptive re-use project in Buffalo's east side.

Ms. Lawson is a past Chair of the New York State Council on the Arts (NYSCA) Special Arts Services Panel, a former member of the Erie County Cultural Resources Advisory Board, a current member of the City of Buffalo Arts Commission, a former City of Buffalo Cultural Review Board panelist and a past Vice Chair of the Cultural Leadership Group which established the Cultural Incentive Funding Program, a demonstration pilot in partnership with State and local funders as well as the Western New York business community. In 1990 and 1991, respectively, she served as Arts Committee Co-Chair and Chair of First Night Buffalo's annual city-wide drug-free cultural celebration.

She has served as a site evaluator for the National Endowment for the Arts (NEA) Expansion Arts Program and on a NEA Challenge Panel. Ms. Lawson also has served on NYSCA's Technical Assistance Committee, the Buffalo Philharmonic Orchestra Marketing Committee, the 1990 *Curtain Up!* Entertainment Committee, and is a founding member of the Buffalo City Ballet Auxiliary Guild.

Celeste is a Board member of Project FLIGHT, a literacy program, and is a member of the steering committee for the Western New York Family Literacy Consortium. She was appointed as a delegate to the United Nations' Non-governmental Organizations (NGO) Region Five European Economic Commission Conference held in Vienna, Austria, in 1994. She also was one of eleven women delegates to the

International Women's Conference held in Beijing, China in 1995. She and delegation members presented on family literacy, cultural and social economic development, and adaptive reuse of historic properties.

Other local activities include her service as Co-Chair and Chair respectively of the United Way's Women in Governance Project in 1999 and 2000. This project prepares women for service on non-profit boards of directors. She has been a member of the Jubilee Fund board, a program that assists the non-profit community with financial assistance through low interest loans. She is an elected Vice President of the Board of the Western New York Grantmakers Association, and served three years on the Leadership Buffalo Board of Directors, of which she also is a 1995 graduate. In 1997, Celeste was elected to the Board of Directors of the New York State Alliance of Arts Organizations. Celeste also was elected to the Board of Directors of the Atlantic Corridor, where she serves on the Cultural Committee. The Atlantic Corridor is an organization whose mission is to develop trade business, educational opportunities, cultural exchanges, and technological relationships in nations along the Atlantic Ocean. In December 2000, Buffalo Mayor Anthony M. Masiello appointed her to the Board of Directors of the Market Arcade Film and Art Center.

Ms. Lawson came to Buffalo after living in Michigan, Georgia, and Western Europe where she spent her formative years. She graduated from the Frankfurt American High School in Frankfurt, Germany, and from the Liberal Arts Program of the Stratton Academy and College in Bedford, England. Since moving to Buffalo in the late 1970s, she completed Bryant and Stratton's Secretarial Administration Program; courses in grant and proposal writing from Canisius College; the Public Relations, Advertising, and Marketing certification program from Millard Fillmore College at the State University of New York at Buffalo; Modern and Ethnic dance courses from SUNY at Buffalo, where she also taught dance classes as part of the Millard Fillmore Lifelong Learning Program; and Arts Administration at Empire State College.

An important part of Ms. Lawson's life is writing poetry and fiction. She writes with the Women of the Crooked Circle, a well-published group of Buffalo women writers. In April 1997 she published a collection of poems reflecting her visit to Beijing, China called *I Was Born This Way*. That same year, she was the featured poet for National Poetry Month and National Library Week in a program sponsored by the American Urban Libraries Program and the American Academy of Poets. The series was called 30-30-30 (30 readings in 30 days in 30 cities). She is a contributing writer for *Her* magazine, a publication that focuses on women's issues and a columnist with *Artvoice*. Celeste is a popular local poet, and is a regular anchor reader with Just Buffalo Literary Center. Her poetry has appeared in *The Buffalo News*, *Earth's Daughters* and other publications.

Shirley Sarmiento

Shirley Sarmiento earned a Master of Arts degree from the State University of New York at Buffalo in 2000. She is the Co-founder/Producer of Buffalo Urban Arts and has worked with over 100 unknown, upcoming local artists of various mediums to evolve their individual projects and complete them for public viewing. She also has arranged readings, performances, and workshops for the artists.

Ms. Sarmiento's professional and literary accomplishments are extensive. Her screenplay, *Tolley's Place*, was selected for the second round at the 2002 Sundance Film Festival. She taught the Coppertown Writer's Workshop at the Langston Hughes Institute and was recruited to be a host for the International Women's Playwrights Conference in Buffalo. She worked in casting for the major motion picture *The Natural* which was filmed in Buffalo. In addition, she is editor of Urban Arts' first anthology, *Drum Beats*. In 1999, she produced her first play, *The Meeting*, at Hallwalls' Black 'n Blue Theater. She has organized numerous poetry group, rap readings, and plays in alternative places throughout Buffalo and Western New York. Ms. Sarmiento also received the 1999 New York State Arts Council individual artist's award.

Prior to the above-referenced work, she was a product of the CETA program where she developed her outreach and recruitment skills as an orator (rapper). She spent several years as a community health worker responsible for counseling youth and families.

She has several works in progress including two plays, a film, several short stories, and has submitted her autobiography, *2Black and 2Powerful*, for publication review.

In 1980, Ms. Sarmiento worked at the battered women's shelter, Haven House, where she counseled abused women and their children and advocated for families in the courtroom. She was a Peace Advocate Educator and conducted a program on alternatives to the military for city and suburban high schools. Through the Peace Center she became a national committee member at the American Friends Service Committee in Philadelphia, Pennsylvania. She is very active in the community and continues to volunteer for numerous agencies.

She has organized lectures and workshops at Orleans Public Library, Canisius College, Gloria J. Parks Community Center, Hallwalls, Inc., Burchfield-Penny Art Center, WBNY-FM radio, Wendy Correctional Facility, Just Buffalo Literary Center, Inc., and Gemini, Inc.

Ms. Sarmiento is the mother of a daughter who is studying to become a librarian. She also has two grandsons, Damiko and Joshua.

Uncrowned Queens in Business

Ruby Butts

Ruby Butts was born on November 25, 1905, in Hogansville, Georgia. She attended Spellman College in Atlanta and the University at Buffalo.

After earning her degrees, Ruby lived in Ashville, North Carolina, where she taught cosmetology at the Alien Home Methodist School for Girls. She also operated a successful beauty and hairdressing business.

In 1937, she moved to Niagara Falls, New York, with her two daughters, Hortense and Gloria, to join her husband, George, who had taken up residence one year prior.

After residing for little more than a year in Niagara Falls, the Butts family moved to Buffalo. Within a short time, Mrs. Butts enrolled her daughters in the Sunday School of the historic Michigan Avenue Baptist Church, pastored by the Reverend J. Edward Nash. Mrs. Butts not only took her children to Sunday school, she became one of its finest teachers, and was ultimately made Sunday School superintendent, a position which she held for several years.

As a community activist, Mrs. Butts served on the City's Human Relations Council; ran for public office, once; was president of the Buffalo Chapter of the National Association of Negro Business and Professional Women's Clubs, Inc. (NANBPW); was one of ten nationally appointed regional organizers for NANBPW during the early 1970s; founded the Sojourner Truth Club to provide services and programs for local young women; and was a member of the Book-Lover's Club. Among her many recognitions are the *Sojourner Truth National Award* and the *Community Service Award* presented by the University at Buffalo.

For approximately thirty-five years, Mrs. Butts owned and operated a beauty and hairdressing salon in Buffalo. She started the business in her home on Clinton Street. Later she moved the business to Jefferson Avenue near Ferry Street. She loved hair design, but she also had great concern and interest in health issues, especially as they affected African American people. As a result, she slowly began to sell "health-food" products at her salon. It was while on Jefferson

Avenue that she decided to expand on her knowledge of cultural variations in nutrition and health care and took two trips around the world as a member of the World Vegetarian Congress. She made visits to Africa, India, and Europe. Her· health business was known as The Healthful Food Shoppe and it was the first business of its kind in Buffalo that was operated by and for African Americans. Finally, she gave up the salon and concentrated solely on her health-food business. Its last location was 19 E. Utica Street, where a housing complex has been named in her honor by the Buffalo and Erie County Community Action Organization (CAO).

Mrs. Butts died in 2000 at the age of ninety-four.

Barbara D. Glover

Barbara Glover has owned and operated her own dance studio in Buffalo for thirty-five years and is certified to teach by Dance Masters of America, Inc. She is founder and president of the Miss Young, Gifted, and Black Pageant that is devoted to promoting the wholesome growth and character development of young African American women.

Ms. Glover was born in Buffalo and educated in Buffalo Public Schools, Niagara County Community College, Bryant and Stratton Business Institute, and Medaille College. She is a 1979 graduate of John Robert Powers Career School.

She has studied dance locally with Fred Jones and Beverly Fletcher; and nationally with Henry LeTang, Jo Jo Smith, Alvin Ailey American Dance Theater, Luigi, and Phil Black. She spent one month in Dakar, Senegal, and The Gambia studying the art of African dance. Her long and varied performing career started at an early age and included several regional theater productions. She has taught, staged, choreographed, directed and/or produced shows for numerous civic, church, and community organizations. She has been guest artist and consultant for the Buffalo Public School System and has choreographed and/or directed musicals at Kensington High School, McKinley High School, and Nardin Academy. She was the teacher and coach of 1972s Miss Black Teenage New York State and Miss Black Teenage America pageants. She has judged numerous competitions including preliminaries for the Miss America Pageant.

She is the recipient of the *Martin Luther King, Jr. Cultural-Enrichment Award* (1976); *Harriet B. Tubman Cultural Award* (1980); Langston Hughes Institute *African American Distinguished Arts Award* (1982); Alpha Kappa Alpha Sorority, Inc., *Excellence in the Arts Award* (1988); Buffalo Public Schools *Quality Integrated Education Award* for outstanding contribution to the promotion of intercultural relations through excellence in the field of dance (1989); *Black Achievers in Industry Award* (1990); African American Police Association *Community Service Award* (1990); Alpha Kappa Alpha Sorority, Inc., *Community Artist Award* (1996); Jack and Jill of America, Inc. *Distinguished Mother Award* (1996); and numerous other awards, citations, felicitations, and proclamations. She was nominated by her peers for the Dance Teacher of the Year and the 2000 Dance Hall of Fame Awards.

Barbara has held membership in the NAACP; National Society of Literature and the Arts; Dance Masters of America, Inc.; National Association of Dance and Affiliated Artists, Inc.; Dance Educators of America, Inc.; National Association of Negro Business and Professional Women's Clubs, Inc.; Erie County Chapter of The Links, Incorporated; and Jack and Jill of America, Inc.

She is the mother of Jayme and Janine, and grandmother of Heavyn Nyri.

June W. Hoeflich

June W. Hoeflich is a senior vice president and commercial executive of HSBC Business Credit (USA) Inc., the Commercial Finance Division of HSBC Bank USA, where she manages the asset based lending, marketing, credit, and portfolio management activities of the Midwest/Upstate New York region. Previously, she was the vice president and manager of the bank's Commercial Loan Underwriting Department, a bank-wide credit unit for financial analysis, loan underwriting, and preparation of credit approval documents.

Ms. Hoeflich began her banking career approximately twenty-five years ago at HSBC Bank USA (formerly Marine Midland Bank) as a clerical instructor. From there she went into branch banking at Manufacturers Hanover. She later entered the Loan Officer's Development Program at Manufacturers and Traders Trust Company. After eight years as a commercial lending officer, she returned to HSBC Bank as a credit training instructor. She later took a two-year assignment in Syracuse, New York, as a district commercial manager for a group of middle market lending officers and then returned to Buffalo to manage HSBC Bank's Financial Business Training Department.

Ms. Hoeflich obtained a Master's degree in business administration with a concentration in finance from Canisius College, after obtaining a Bachelor's in business from the University at Buffalo and an Associate's degree in business from Erie Community College.

She is very active in community, professional, and charitable organizations. Ms. Hoeflich is on the International Board of Directors of the Credit Risk Management Association. She also has the following affiliations: international chairperson for RMA's Professional Development Council; board of advisors for the Buffalo Federation of Neighborhood Centers, Inc.; member of the University at Buffalo's Business Alliance; board member of the Erie Community College Foundation; chairperson of St. Gregory the Great's Strategic Planning Committee; treasurer of Grace Manor Health Care Facility board; and a founding member of the Buffalo Chapter, National Association of Urban Bankers. She also is an active participant in various philanthropic and cultural organizations.

Annie Pearl McSpadden

Annie Pearl McSpadden is a graduate of Lillian Dora and the Buffalo School of Beauty Culture. She has been a licensed, practicing cosmetologist for over forty years.

As proprietor and operator of the *Feminess Beauty Salon*, she employs two cosmetologists. She also is a partner of *LaBoutique*. She is an instructor for BOCES on-the-job training programs. In order to continue her professional development, Annie Pearl participates in numerous educational and cosmetology seminars throughout the year including those in Greensboro, North Carolina, and Jamaica's Hilton Head, South Carolina. Her achievements in the field of cosmetology have been recognized by community organizations through receipt of several awards for hair-cutting, years of service, and diversity of salon services.

She attended Medaille College and pursued a degree in Business Administration.

Her civic affiliations include the Frontier Chapter of the American Business Woman Association, Buffalo Chamber of Congress, and Albright-Knox Art Gallery. Her community service activities include modeling for cancer awareness shows, volunteering as a panelist on television cancer awareness programming, and providing support for women diagnosed with breast cancer through the Life After Breast Cancer committee. She is a yearly sponsor of children at the YMCA. In addition, she is a member of St. John Baptist Church where she has served on the Adult Usher Board and volunteered for the Good Shepard Society and Sunday School.

She is an avid sports enthusiast having participated in and won awards for golfing tournaments. Her other activities include swimming, reading, and watching football, basketball, and golf events on television. Her hobbies include collecting clowns, calligraphy, and finding good in everyone she meets.

Annie Pearl is the wife of Melvin McSpadden; mother of Roshelle L. Lewis (Essentino, Sr.); and grandmother of Essentino, Jr., John D., and Melissa Lewis. She also is a great-grandmother.

Ann Montgomery

Ann Montgomery Woodson was born in Americus, Georgia. When she was an infant, her parents moved to Los Angeles, California. She attended school in Los Angeles as well as in Texas before moving to Buffalo, New York, in 1910.

Shortly after her arrival in Buffalo, Ann opened an ice cream parlor at 496 Michigan Avenue, which would later become the location of the Little Harlem. She operated the ice cream parlor until the early 1920s when she established the Oriental Billiard Parlor. A few years later she converted this business into the Little Harlem Hotel and nightclub. Mrs. Montgomery began the cabaret that initiated the nightclub in 1934. In the early days, the Little Harlem became a major showcase for aspiring new stars during an era when it was difficult for them to obtain jobs in their professions elsewhere. The roster of stars included both black and white performers such as Louis Armstrong, Billie Holliday, Bing Crosby, Vincent Lopez, Cab Calloway, and Dinah Washington, among the more popular names who performed at or visited the hotel and club. The nightspot also became a meeting ground for political and elected officials. As noted in her obituary, "For many years the Little Harlem Hotel has been considered a landmark in Buffalo and it is believed to be the oldest established black business here."

Mrs. Montgomery was a member of the Buffalo Chapter of the National Association for the Advancement of Colored People (NAACP); the Michigan Avenue YMCA; and the Hadji Court 62, Daughters of Isis. She was known to be a supporter and generous contributor to the Boys Club of America, the Negro College Fund Foundation, the Salvation Army, the United Way of Buffalo and Erie

County, Catholic Charities, the Police Athletic League, and numerous other community and civic organizations.

Ann Montgomery was a remarkable businesswoman. Her death, on April 11, 1978, ended a career that spanned nearly seventy years. Ann's husband, Paul Dilworth Woodson, managed the club for thirty-three years prior to his wife's death. He continued to manage the club for many years until his retirement and the sale of the club to Judge Wilbur Trammell. Unfortunately, the club was destroyed by fire during the 1990s.

Jennifer Parker

Jennifer J. Parker is the present owner and co-founder of the Black Capital Network (*www.thebcn.com*), an informational Web site portal developed to educate, empower, and promote the African American Community. The Web site was designed to address the underexposure of black owned businesses, and to showcase the many talents and services that the African American community has to offer to both local residents and the worldwide community. The Black Capital Network's goal is to fill the gap created by the inability of national black web portals to cover local businesses and community issues. The company provides services such as Web site design, customer databases, Internet hosting, and marketing of Web sites that will enable African American businesses to utilize technology in operating and promoting their businesses. The company plans to offer small business consulting services throughout the United States.

Under Ms. Parker's leadership, the Black Capital Network has hosted small business workshops, networking events, and a business speaker series consisting of national business leaders and motivational speakers highlighting the message of empowerment and cooperative economic success. The company has planned an Economic Empowerment Conference in an effort to highlight the importance of economic development and obtaining the skills necessary to help build successful businesses.

Ms. Parker and the company were featured on the WNED Radio program, *Your Business*, hosted by Lew Mandell, Dean of UB's School of Management, on March 31, 2001, to announce the launch of the Web site. The company has recently introduced a companion Web site entitled *Our Culture.net*, a Web site designed to celebrate and preserve the African American experience and culture.

In 1981, Ms. Parker received her undergraduate degree from Johnson C. Smith University and moved from Charlotte, North Carolina, to Buffalo, New York to attend the University at Buffalo, School of Law. After receiving a Juris Doctorate degree, her professional career was targeted to the field of insurance and personal injury law where she worked in numerous corporate positions including Alternative Dispute Resolution (ADR) Coordinator. As the ADR Coordinator for Travelers Insurance Company's Commercial Liability Unit, she negotiated and resolved numerous liability lawsuits and claims on behalf of major national corporations such as Chase Manhattan Bank, American Express, and Metropolitan Life Insurance Company. Ms. Parker was responsible for organizing and managing New York City Settlement Days in which both arbitrations and mediations were utilized to settle cases. She also created and edited a Newsletter for her department entitled, *Making ADR Work for You.*

Ms. Parker has been certified as a Web Designer and Web Developer through the University at Buffalo, School of Management and continues to seek further certification in cutting edge web technology.

Ms. Parker is married to Melvin A. Parker, a Buffalo attorney, and is the mother of three children.

Sarah Goggins Pittman

Sarah Goggins Pittman is a successful Buffalo-based businesswoman. As a former admissions counselor and student recruiter at Bryant and Stratton, she encouraged and guided hundreds of students through an advanced education.

She entered the job placement field after discovering that a number of minority students were unable to obtain jobs. As a manager of a local secretarial service, she brought the number of employees from five to 125. In 1979, the Buffalo born and raised Mrs. Pittman opened her own firm, Sarette Secretarial Services Inc., and then expanded to the Niagara Falls area in 1982. Later, her husband, Winton "Skip" Pittman, joined the firm as vice president of a new division, Sarette Technical Services.

In five years, 500 people had obtained permanent employment through Sarette and the efforts of the Pittmans and their staff of five.

Mrs. Pittman, a graduate of Bennett Park School No. 32 who attended Bryant and Stratton, believes success can be attained by every person through hard work and sticking to one's dreams and ideals. The youngest of eleven children, she learned from her parents that hard work is the path to recognition and that a belief in God is important to one's life.

Her own efforts to help others achieve success have earned her various awards that include: *Black Business Women of the Year*; *Black Achiever's Award*; and the *Certificate of Merit for Outstanding Achievement and Minority Vendor of the Year* presented by organizations such as *The Buffalo News*, *Buffalo Courier-Express*, the New York State Assembly, and the Upstate Minority Purchasing Council. Governor Mario Cuomo named her to the New York State Department of Commerce Advisory Council for Minority Women in 1984.

Mrs. Pittman and her husband combine business and civic activities with an active family life. They have two daughters.

Lessie Roland

Lessie Arnold was born in Poplar Bluff, Missouri, in 1907. She was the fourth eldest of nine children born to Bernard and Catherine Miller Arnold. While still a child, Lessie moved to Buffalo, New York, with her family. Later the family moved to Cheektowaga, New York, where they lived in an area that is now part of the New York State Thruway. She attended Buffalo Public Schools, but left after completing the eleventh grade to take a job doing domestic work.

She met and married Horace Roland, one of the first black taxi drivers in Buffalo. Together, they had three daughters. The couple and their daughters moved to Bennett Street and often traded with neighborhood stores including Goldstein's Delicatessen located at 258 William Street. Lessie was hired as a clerk in the store, the first African American to work in the business.

During World War II, she went to work at the Curtiss Aircraft Plant on Northland Avenue. Later she operated the food kitchen in Kern's Grill at William and Pratt Street. She was noted for her cooking. During this time, the Goldsteins sold their business to an African American and opened another store in the Cold Spring area.

In the days when numbers gambling was illegal, but people played anyway, Lessie took a chance on the numbers. She won $2500 as a result. Lessie's winning number, 244, was her daughter's hospital room. Later her daughter succumbed to her illness.

The business at 258 William Street had not prospered under its new owners, who put it up for sale. Lessie purchased the business and later she purchased the building that housed it. *Lessie's Delicatessen* was launched as a family owned and managed business. It was known for its fresh, hard to find meat and vegetables. Lessie, her husband and children ran the business for forty-five years.

The business was closed following Horace's death in the late 1970s. Lessie moved to a senior citizen complex. She was still in business, however, as she sold Watkins products out of her apartment. She was still active at age eighty-nine, driving her own car until it was stolen. She did some cooking at the YMCA and planned bus trips to the home of a spiritualist at Lily Dale.

Lessie Arnold Roland was one of the oldest living members of the Lincoln Memorial United Methodist Church celebrating a 75 year membership. She died in 1999 at the age of 92.

Enid Wright

Enid Wright moved to Buffalo in 1956, from the small town of Alcoa, Tennessee. She graduated from Buffalo State College in 1962 with a degree in Elementary Education and received a Master's degree in counseling from the University at Buffalo in 1974.

Enid has left her footprints in the field of education, community activism, and art. From 1962 - 1994 she taught honors classes and counseled students who had special needs at various Buffalo public schools.

Her entrepreneurial spirit and creative talents led her into the art world and for many years her career ran a parallel path as an educator and art dealer. Since 1973, Enid has made countless trips to more than fifteen African countries in search of unique artifacts.

On the community front, she was an active volunteer with the BUILD organization, taking on leadership roles. She is currently a member of the Buffalo Juneteenth of Buffalo, Inc., and Chair of Financial Development.

Her life experiences continue in full stride. She exhibits African art at large festivals, professional conferences, and business expositions.

Ms. Wright is the personification of individualism. She forges her own path while sharing her resources, energy, and talent with those whose path she crosses.

Sylvia Wright

Sylvia Elaine Gethers Wright was one of two children born to Lois and William Gethers in Johnstown, Pennsylvania. In 1956, her family moved to Buffalo, New York, where she has since resided.

After graduating from East High School, she was employed by Blue Shield of Western New York as a Medicare Service Representative before getting married and starting a family. Following the birth of her son, she decided to return to school and enrolled in Erie Community College. She held several jobs in the community, including office manager of the Black Development Foundation, Inc., before being hired by Moog, Inc. as a numerical control computer operator in the methods engineering department. Her career with Moog now spans twenty-four years and she is the first African American in the company to achieve the position of Senior Program Manager. In this capacity, Sylvia manages multi-million dollar programs and travels extensively both domestically and abroad.

While employed at Moog, Sylvia attended night school and earned a Bachelor of Arts degree in Adult Training and Development from Medaille College. She attended the Executive Development Program of the Harvard Business School Club of Buffalo and earned a Master of Science Degree in Global Business from Daemen College. She has served on several committees within the company including the Minority Advisory Committee.

Sylvia is the thirteenth president of the Mary B. Talbert Civic and Cultural Club where she has been an active member since 1992. As a federated woman, Sylvia has the opportunity to serve in the community and reach out to her neighbors, particularly women and children, who need a helping hand. Sylvia is a life member of the National Association of Colored Women's Clubs, Inc. She believes that as a people, we can accomplish everything with love, guidance, and nurturing. She notes, "God has truly been good to me and I pray for continued strength and courage that will allow me to spread his blessings as far as I can reach." This philosophy has garnered her many distinctions and awards.

Sylvia was voted Neighbor of the Year for submitting the first Block Grant proposal to the City of Buffalo for residential lampposts that have since become a beacon of light in the community. She initiated and chaired the Empire State Federation Women of Distinction note card project that commemorates outstanding federated women from New York State, and she currently serves as Vice President of the Empire State Buffalo Region.

In 1998, Sylvia was recognized as Club Woman of the Year by Zonta International Buffalo Club #1. As a member of Zonta, she also was co-organizer of the Lafayette High School Z Club that provides a support network of professional and executive businesswomen helping young women develop leadership skills and reach their full potential.

When possible, Sylvia also enjoys working with young elementary and intermediate school children as a technical advisor for Buffalo-area Engineering Awareness for Minorities (BEAM).

As a member of St. John Baptist Church, Sylvia was co-organizer of St. John Boy Scout Troop #84 and currently serves on the #2 Usher Board.

Sylvia is the mother of a son, Hollice Wood, Jr., daughter-in-law, Yolanda, and the grandmother of Amaya Emon.

Uncrowned Queens in Community and Social Service Organizations

Amelia Grace Anderson

Amelia Grace Anderson was a member of a prominent African American family that settled in Buffalo as early as 1832. She was one of the first blacks to graduate from Syracuse University where she earned a Doctorate in Liberal Arts.

She taught school in Buffalo and was an active member of the National Association of Colored Women's Clubs. Locally, she was one of the founders, with Florence Lee, of the Lit-Mus Study Club in 1922. In 1938, she was elected president of the Empire State Federation of Women's Clubs.

Ms. Anderson was at the forefront of leadership in the establishment of the Buffalo Chapter of the National Association for the Advancement of Colored People. She was one of the Chapter's founders and served as secretary of the organization in 1917. In 1928, she was elected President of the Buffalo NAACP.

She is the aunt of Uncrowned Queen, Ora Anderson Curry, and the sister-in-law of Ora L. Anderson.

Ms. Anderson died on May 31, 1950, and is interred in Forest Lawn Cemetery.

Bettie S. Anderson

A native of Lynchburg, Virginia, Mrs. Anderson was a graduate of Hampton Institute (now Hampton University). She taught at an elementary school near Lynchburg until her marriage to Mack G. Anderson in 1893, when the newlyweds moved to New York City. The couple had four children and the family came to Buffalo in 1908. Soon after their arrival, Mack Anderson established Buffalo's first black hotel, the Manhattan Hotel.

Mrs. Anderson soon became actively involved as a member of the Michigan Avenue Baptist Church where she became a friend of Mary B. Talbert. They sponsored youth programs and taught Sunday School. As her church activities continued, she was elected church clerk and served in that office from 1922-1943. In the early thirties, she became a member of the Deaconess Board. During the Depression years of the thirties, the church organized a group known as the Prosperity Club, a social group of men and women that assisted in fundraising for the church.

As the years went by, Mrs. Anderson became more involved in the community. She was an early member of the Phyllis Wheatley Club of Colored Women and also became active in the Federation of Colored Women's Clubs. These two organizations sponsored cultural programs such as musical teas, lectures, dramatic presentations, art exhibits, and social activities. A member of the Naomi Chapter of the Eastern Stars, she held several offices and became Worthy Matron about 1932.

Having observed a number of friends becoming ill and needing care, she became interested in nursing. The first minority person enrolled in the American Red Cross Home Nursing course, she received certification from the national office. This led to some part-time volunteer care of local patients in their homes.

An early supporter of the Buffalo Urban League, she was an active volunteer assisting in the promotion of many special events. She also worked in a small community center that had been organized by the YMCA in the Prudy Street area. Mrs. Anderson joined in working with a parents club to encourage the leadership of youth programs and their sponsorship of annual outdoor carnivals.

Because of declining health, Mrs. Anderson had terminated many of her activities in the early forties. She died in 1948 at the age of 81.

Mrs. Anderson is related to two other Uncrowned Queens. She is the mother of Theresa G. Evans, and grandmother of Theresa's daughter, Gwendolyn Greene.

Ruth Bryant

A native of Ellenville, New York, Ruth came to Buffalo to attend the University at Buffalo, which was a private institution. Following graduation from UB, her family told her that she could remain in Buffalo if she obtained employment. Opportunities in the mid- to late 1960s were limited to young woman of color, but sensing that job growth was possible at her alma mater, and being true to the advise of her elders in securing employment, Ruth began her long tenure at the University.

She is an administrator, involved in both University and community activities, and a political activist. In 1982, she was appointed Assistant Dean in the School of Architecture and Planning where she was responsible for all human resource-related activities as well as school-wide events. She was the first person of color to be elected Chair of the Professional Staff Senate (1988), the governing body for professionals at the University at Buffalo. She has served on university-wide committees including the Task Force on Women at UB, Faculty Senate Committee on Governance, and numerous search committees. She also has been active SUNY-wide in faculty governance.

Her community activities include the following: current Chair of the Board of the Community Foundation for Greater Buffalo; Chair, Board of Directors for the Reverend Dr. Bennett W. Smith, Sr., Family Life Center; and Chair, Board of Directors HELP, Buffalo. Other board memberships include Local Initiatives Support Corporation; Co-Chair of United Neighborhoods; Education Fund for Greater Buffalo; Rental Assistance Corporation and Housing Development Corporation; and for nine years, United Way of New York State (Secretary, 1996-2000). Her immediate past board activities include the Board of Trustees for Medaille College, the Erie County Cultural Resources Advisory Board, and the YWCA of Western New York.

The YWCA, Everywoman Opportunity Center, National Conference, NAACP, Black Achievers, and the University at Buffalo have honored Ruth with awards for her community service.

A political activist, Ruth has been an elected committee person and is a member of Woman's PAC, which supports local women running for elective office. Her neighborhood involvement includes Chairperson of the Willert Park Village Community Association, a neighborhood that has won national awards for its redevelopment, and appointment by Mayor Anthony M. Masiello to chair the Ellicott District Planning Council (2002).

A founding member of the Buffalo Chapter of the National Coalition of 100 Black Women, Ms. Bryant believes one of her roles is to mentor and share her knowledge with others.

Ms. Bryant is an active member of St. John Baptist Church where she serves on numerous committees.

She is married to Earl Lynch and is the stepparent to three adult children and grandparent of Aisha and Aidan.

Earline Collier

Earline Audrey Tillman-Collier, a young and energetic mother of two children, Darryl LaRue and Sibyl Pearl, joined her husband, Tolliver, in Buffalo from Houston, Texas. In less than one year, she was a volunteer substituting for the pianist at the Calvary Baptist Church where the Reverend Peter Trammel was Pastor.

Her family lived on Cedar Street across from the Buffalo Urban League where she became an active volunteer. She had a brief working relationship with the Women's Guild during the presidency of Cora P. Maloney.

In the early 1950s, Mrs. Collier and Genevieve Kelly were two of seven women who founded the Bronze Damsels Civic, Philanthropic Social Club. These dynamic women made a significant cultural difference in the city and were first to honor and spotlight "First Blacks" such as Ensa Poston, the first black Civil Service Commissioner of New York State; Dr. George Blackman, the first black Surgeon at Roswell Park Cancer Institute; Dr. Claude Clapp, the first black Assistant Principal of a Buffalo Public School; Arthur O. Eve, the first black Deputy Speaker of the New York State Assembly;

Eddie Ownes, the first black Manager of National Fuel; Jacqueline Curry, the first black Air Traffic Controller; and many more. Under Earline's leadership the Club paid a semester's tuition at Nichols School for a gifted, intelligent, young black student.

Her community service continued as she chaired many important committees. As president of the Women's Auxiliary of the Buffalo Branch NAACP, she expanded the group from fifty to sixty members, organized a potluck fundraiser that was attended by more than three hundred people, and held another major fundraiser in the Top of the Town Restaurant. The Auxiliary also was responsible for the Fight for Freedom Fund Assessment.

Earline also chaired an ad-hoc committee to raise funds for the United Negro College Fund and presented a $5,000 check to the organization on the Channel 4 UNCF telethon. She chaired a committee called *Surviving the 1977 Blizzard* to raise funds for 1490 Senior Center. She also created a mail-a-thon to various clubs that sought donations to purchase a fax machine for the Center.

Mrs. Tillman-Collier was the co-founder of the Harriet Tubman 300s and served as president for twenty-one years. Under her leadership this group of ladies hosted many community events and endeavored to perpetuate the spirit of Harriet Tubman.

She served for five years on the advisory board of the New York State Office of the Aging and was the Western New York African American delegate to the White House Conference on Aging. She filled Kleinhan's Music Hall twice as the *Hypothermia Lady*, teaching seniors how to survive hot or cold weather.

Earline was an excellent leader who worked endlessly to achieve her goals. She was a much sought-after Women's Day Speaker and fashion commentator. She was a Task Force member working to establish the Erie County Commission on the Status of Women and also served as Chair of the Erie County Department of Senior Service Advisory Board.

Mrs. Tillman-Collier was recognized and honored by numerous community, civic, governmental, and human service organizations such as the Phyllis Wheatley Club of Colored Women, Mary B. Talbert award; Sojourner Truth (Business and Professional Women); Alpha Kappa Alpha Sorority, Inc., Gamma Phi Omega Chapter; Zeta Phi Beta Inter Club Council; University at Buffalo University Women; YWCA; Bethel Church (Human Service) Black Educators Association;

NAACP (Human Relations); Network on Aging (New York State); Bison Assembly #48; Zonta Club of Amherst; and Lincoln Memorial United Methodist Church.

Stephanie Lynn Williams Cowart

Stephanie Lynn Williams Cowart was born in Niagara Falls, New York. She is the seventh of nine children born to Ada and James Williams.

She attended Niagara Falls public schools including Beech Avenue, North Junior, and Niagara Falls High School. Upon graduation, she continued her education at Niagara University earning a Bachelor of Science degree in Commerce Management, a Bachelor of Arts degree in Accounting, and a Master's degree in Business Administration. She also is a Certified Public Housing Manager and graduate of Leadership Niagara. In addition, she is pursuing a Certification in Executive Director Leadership.

Ms. Cowart is Executive Director for the Niagara Falls Housing Authority, having been employed there for seventeen years.

An active member of Mount Zion Missionary Baptist Church, she serves as Choir Director, Trustee, President of the James L. Williams Memorial Scholarship Fund Committee, and Advisor for the Junior Ushers Youth Group. She actively promotes, organizes, and participates in Women Fellowship Programs/Activities and is a member of various other ad hoc committees. Stephanie is a founding member of the Niagara Falls Music Workshop Choir.

She is an active member of Delta Sigma Theta Sorority, Inc., and the Niagara Falls Chapter of The Links, Incorporated.

Other professional affiliations include: Member of Fleet Advisory Board; Member of the Task Force on the Status of Women in Niagara County; Trustee, Niagara Educational Foundation; Niagara Falls Board of Education School to Work Preparation Committee; Niagara Falls High School Diversity Implementation Team; Niagara County Community College Business Advisory Committee; Public Housing Authorities Director's Association Scholarship and Professional Development Committees; Central New York Housing Authorities;

National Association of Housing and Redevelopment Officials; the Center for the Stabilization of the Black Family; and the National Association for the Advancement of Colored People.

Ms. Cowart is the recipient of numerous awards including the Niagara County Black Achiever's *Candle in the Dark Award*, Niagara Improvement Association *Civic Award*, Niagara University *Fellowship Award*, Niagara Falls Housing Authority *Award of Excellence*, *Business First*'s prestigious *Forty Under 40* award, Niagara County's *Woman of the Year Award*, and *Heroes of Public Housing Award*. She also is listed in *Who's Who of Professionals*.

Ms. Cowart currently resides in Grand Island with her husband and two children.

Barbara Kirkland Dennis

Barbara Kirkland Dennis is a native of Buffalo who, for more than twenty-five years, has demonstrated a sincere commitment to family and community restoration. Her dedication in this field of work is a result of the experiences in her own life.

She attended Buffalo P.S. #32, P.S. #31, and East High School. She graduated from the BOCES/New York State School for Practical Nursing in 1965. Later she went on to earn a Bachelor of Science degree from Empire State College in Community and Human Services Substance Abuse Counseling in addition to an Applied Sciences degree in Social Sciences.

As a divorced mother with three teenagers and a three-year-old toddler, she sought assistance in providing direction for her sixteen-year-old son who had not committed a crime. She, like many other African American mothers, pursued a more traditional path to seek Family Court help. Barbara, like other mothers, didn't have a clear understanding of adolescent crisis, nor did she think that the justice system that she had asked for help would be so uncaring and destructive to her family. She notes that her experiences in life have really been an education towards gaining her freedom. She also feels she has obtained a doctorate degree via the *University of Hard Knocks*.

As if in the spirit of Sojourner Truth, Barbara would not accept just herself being free.

Thus, Barbara, a Human Service provider and a highly motivated individual, has effectively advocated for families since 1976. She became the first resident and member of the Kensington-Bailey Neighborhood Housing Services to be elected President of its Board of Directors after her efforts brought forth more than four hundred new residents and members. In addition, she became the relentless motivational force behind the creation and implementation of the first New York State Division for Youth's Family Advocacy Component at Masten Park's Community Involvement Program.

By 1980, Barbara had founded M.O.T.I.C., Mothers Of Those In Crisis. Ms. Dennis became the forerunner in Family Advocacy and Restoration as she addressed the issues of injustice in the Justice System. M.O.T.I.C. is a self-supported group of female heads of households with family members involved in the court system at every level. M.O.T.I.C. members are dedicated, skilled volunteers who share and work with each other and others in healing from and dealing with the pain, sorrow, destruction, and devastation of losing a member to the Criminal Justice System.

Barbara's accomplishments are many. She was the first African American to be Infirmary nurse at the Erie County Jail/Holding Center. Her civic and social activities include: African American Issues delegate (1993); implementer of Children First Adopting a New Covenant on Behalf of the Next Generation; African World Youth and Young Adult Conference; Alternatives to Incarceration Task Force; Buffalo Community Partnership Coalition; Buffalo Substance Abuse Prevention Coalition; Erie County Legislatures City/County Crime Task Force/Family Restoration; Genesee Humboldt Junior High School Self Enrichment Program; Masten Park Community Involvement Program; National Association of Sentencing Advocates, Washington, D.C.; Neighborhood Housing Services of Buffalo Inc.; South Park High School - Community Educator and Parent Advisory Council; The Sentencing Project Washington, D.C.; Urban Christian Ministry; and the Youth Planning Council of the Near East Side.

Susan Evans

Susan Evans was a college-educated social worker who attended higher education in Chicago and trained at a settlement house there.

In 1899, she co-founded the Phyllis Wheatley Club of Colored Women in Buffalo and was the club's first president. She gave the official welcome address to members of the National Association of Colored Women's Clubs when it held its second biennial conference in Buffalo in July 1901 during the Pan American Exposition of 1901. Mrs. Evans was elected as the organization's National Recording Secretary at this conference. She later directed the settlement house that the Phyllis Wheatley Club of Colored Women founded in Buffalo in 1905.[1]

Theresa G. Evans

Born in New York City, Theresa G. Evans came to Buffalo in 1908 with her parents, Mack Gordon Anderson and Bettie Spencer Anderson, and her two brothers. Her father established the Manhattan Hotel on Michigan Avenue.

She was a graduate of a local public school and the Bryant and Stratton Business College. She studied at Northwestern University School of Office Management and the University at Buffalo, The State University of New York.

Employed first at the M. Wile Company as a certified accountant, she later married William James Greene, Jr., and lived in Baltimore, Maryland, for several years before returning to Buffalo.

One of the first two staff members employed at the Buffalo Urban League when it was founded in 1927, Mrs. Evans had advanced to become the Executive Assistant. In 1948, she married Williams L. Evans, then Executive Director of the League. She helped the League

---

[1] Williams, Lillian. "And Still I Rise: Black Women and Reform – Buffalo, New York 1900-1940." *Afro-Americans in New York Life and History.* Vol. 14, No. 6 (1990) 7-33.

develop its broad program and supported it as an honorary member of its Board of Directors. She retired from the League in 1964.

Mrs. Evans served community youth as a member of the Girl Scout Council, YWCA Board, and as a fundraiser for both agencies. She was an active member of the Advisory Board of the Salvation Army for more than twenty years, and she was a member of the United Way House of Delegates. Because of her added interest in elderly persons, she was appointed secretary of the Senior Aides Program of Buffalo's Research and Planning Council where she served for two years.

Since few black women were employed in business during the Depression years, Mrs. Evans banded together with several other qualified women to found the Buffalo Chapter of Iota Phi Lambda business sorority. She also was a charter member of the Buffalo Chapter of The Links, Incorporated, a national service organization.

As a member of Lincoln Memorial United Methodist Church, she belonged to the Wesleyan Guild, the Commission on Missions, and continued activity with United Methodist Women. She was the oldest member of her church.

She served as organist of the Michigan Avenue Baptist Church for over twenty years and was blessed with a beautiful, rich contralto voice that was often combined in duets with others including her sister-in-law, the late Lauretta Anderson, former choirmaster of Lincoln Memorial United Methodist Church.

Mrs. Evans is the mother of another Uncrowned Queen, Gwendolyn Greene.

She was ninety-nine years old at the time of her death on November 19, 1999.

Rosa Gibson

Rosa Gibson was educated at Carver High School in Detroit, Michigan. She earned an Associate's degree from the School of Nursing at Niagara County Community College and a Bachelor of Science degree in Nursing from D'Youville College.

She is a determined woman with a deep sense of community, turning her Best Street home into a crime fighting headquarters to help launch a system of neighborhood patrols by and for the people. She organized the City of Buffalo's first nighttime citizen's patrols. As President of the Masten Park Community Block Club No. 1, she became leader of the club's Crime Watch Program, which put volunteer patrols on some of the toughest city streets in search of suspicious activity to report to the police. This led to a Night Out for Masten Park, a program that encouraged area residents to turn on their house lights, sit on their front porches, and talk to their neighbors to show support for the fight against crime. Her organization is responsible for holding Buffalo's first National Night Out. The program was such a success that it went city-wide in 1984. The Crime Watch program that she oversees also is concerned about monitoring trash dumping and abandoned houses in the neighborhood.

Ms. Gibson has fought against many injustices for area citizens including the imposing of a garbage user fee by the City of Buffalo. She also got the city to replace traffic lights and street signs on several area streets.

As the President and Director of the Community Action Information Center, Inc. (CAIC), Ms. Gibson's activities are extensive. CAIC deals with any problem that may arise in the community from improper traffic sign demarcation to hazardous materials dumping. Ms. Gibson coordinates and administers several target projects under the auspices of CAIC. She runs a food shelter that picks up food items from various stores and makes monthly deliveries to senior citizens. Through the Crime Watch Patrolling Project, Ms. Gibson, and other volunteers, work closely with the Buffalo Police Department to report any illegal street activities, including gangs, illegal drugs, and vacant housing.

In addition to the above projects, she coordinates and supervises staff and volunteers in the COURTS and HIRE programs. Through the COURTS program, workers are sent by the Buffalo City Court to do community service in lieu of serving time in jail. The HIRE Program disseminates workers throughout the community to work for their stipend from the Department of Social Services. Ms. Gibson supervises Senior Aid Program workers who are fifty-five years of age and over and are referred to work for Center Supportive Services. She also supervises and coordinates the Neighborhood Youth Task Force that enables young people to help identify community needs, participate in various community activities, and take education tours.

Currently, Ms. Gibson is working to inform the public about the purchase and proposed usage of 485 Best Street, the former Youth Detention Facility. The state sold this cavernous structure to the Islamic Society of America (ISA). The Society plans to convert the complex into a mosque, school, and boarding school. Ms. Gibson's primary concern centers on the issue of the safe removal of the razor sharp barbed wire that was placed around the top of the building when it was an active detention center. She is seeking to promote an open dialogue between the Islamic Society of America and the community that surrounds the building.

Ms. Gibson coordinates community beautification projects to clean vacant lots, decorate streets during the holidays, make sure garbage is picked up, assure abandoned houses are maintained, and abandoned cars are removed from the street. She also coordinates the planning and cultivation of community gardens in vacant city lots for vegetables for the community. On a larger scale, CAIC is part of the Victory Gardens Partnership Project that works to transform vacant city lots into evergreen forests, fruit orchards, and butterfly and memorial gardens for the community to share and enjoy. The Buffalo Museum of Science, Stanley Makowski Early Childhood Center, and Sandy White from the City of Buffalo, along with student volunteers from the University at Buffalo, are assisting with these projects.

Her memberships include the Prince of Peace Temple Church of God in Christ, Inc.; United Neighborhood Advisory Board; Buffalo Public Schools Space Utilization Task Force; Citizens Against Tax; and Crime Watch Program.

Gwendolyn Greene

Gwendolyn Greene is a native Buffalonian who attended local public schools. She earned a Bachelor of Arts degree from Virginia State University and a Master of Social Work degree from the University of Pittsburgh. Ms. Greene completed additional coursework at both the University of Michigan and University at Buffalo.

She worked as a group worker for the Buffalo Urban League. Following this position, she was Program Director in Residential Treatment of disturbed children for the Children's Aid Society (Child and Family Services). She also was Program Director for the Huntington House of Syracuse where she was assigned to the organization's family group work agency. In addition, she served as Director of Service to military families and veterans at the Buffalo chapter of the American Red Cross.

Ms. Greene is a member of the Trustee Board of the American Red Cross, Buffalo Chapter, and the Board of the Afro-American Historical Association of the Niagara Frontier, Inc. She is a member of the National Association of Social Workers; and is past Director of the YWCA Youth Department that served all area high school clubs. She was selected by the National YWCA to participate in the Latin-American/USA project to do leadership exchange in four South American countries. In this capacity she was responsible for training.

Finally, she served as a board member of the Child Care Council, the YWCA, the Council of Churches, Gateway Home for Children, Camp Fire Boys and Girls (President), the National Board - Camp Fire Boys and Girls, the National Board - American Red Cross Retirees Association, and the Trustee Boards of Lincoln Memorial United Methodist Church and Humboldt Parkway Baptist Church.

In addition to being listed in *Who's Who of American Women* and *Who's Who of American Service Professionals*, Ms. Greene has received numerous service and appreciation awards including the Buffalo Common Council *Award for Community Service*; Camp Fire Council, *Friend of Children Award*; YWCA, *Professional Service Award*; Children's Aid Society, *Outstanding Performance Award*; Buffalo Urban League, *Professional Award for Service to Youth in Treatment*; NAACP, *Human*

Relations Award; NCCJ, *Brotherhood Award for Community Service*; Delta Sigma Theta Sorority, Inc. award for fifty years of service; Camp Fire *National Board Service Award*; Boy Scout Council *Appreciation Award*; American Red Cross *Appreciation Award*; Buffalo Museum of Science *Appreciation Award*; and the YWCA *Volunteer Award*. She also was a recipient of the *William Wells Brown Award* from the Afro-American Historical Association of the Niagara Frontier, Inc.

Ms. Greene is related to two other Uncrowned Queens. She is the daughter of Theresa G. Evans, and the granddaughter of Bettie S. Anderson.

Mary Hackney

Give her of the fruits of her hands and let her own works praise her in the gates.
Proverbs 31:31

Mrs. Mary J. Hackney was a survivor. She lived through the Great Depression on Buffalo's east side by knowing how to sew, grow food in her garden, and smile. Daughter of the late Edward and Hattie McCurry, she was born in Memphis, Tennessee, on May 22, 1903.

"I knew how to manipulate. I could buy five cents worth of potatoes, five cents worth of carrots, and five cents worth of beef and I always had something to put back in the ice box. I could take five cents worth of apples, put some brown sugar with them and we had dessert too."

She was baptized when she was thirteen years old at Salem Baptist Church in Memphis. She came to Buffalo in 1921, and joined the Trinity Baptist Church where she worked faithfully for sixty-nine years. She held positions such as Sunday School Teacher for over sixty years, Missionary Society President for twelve years, President of the Women's Auxiliary for nine years (a charter member receiving fifteen year service pin in April 1969), President of the Women's Auxiliary New England State Convention for five years, and President of the Church Women United of Buffalo and Erie County for two years, and was a pianist when needed. Her motto was, "To Serve This Present Age."

She graduated from Hutchinson Central High School and aspired to be a Foreign Missionary Worker. She studied Sunday school administration, Old and New Testament doctrine, personal evangelism and pedagogy at the Buffalo Bible Institute (now Houghton College). She took evening courses in Anthropology, Physiology, and Sociology at the University at Buffalo.

Her marriage to the late Deacon John Hackney was the first wedding performed at the Trinity Baptist Church. Together with her husband, they raised six children (three boys and three girls).

In recalling the Depression, she said, "I had the education, but my husband had the good common sense." She explained her husband wanted her children to be educated and that she read to them from the newspaper and gave them lectures on the importance of going to school.

In 1952, she was chosen *Mother of the Year* in the Ellicott District and given a citation from Mayor Joseph Murck. In 1962, Mayor Chester Kowal gave her the City's *Good Neighbor Award*.

She volunteered her services to the American Red Cross, hospitals, and schools and worked with the Conference of Christians and Jews and the Erie County Recreation Board.

She was a world traveler – visiting over thirty countries. Pan American Airlines complimented her. She traveled with an American Baptist Group that was led by the late Dr. Ralph Johnson of Berkley Divinity School.

During her World Tour she wrote articles for *The Buffalo News* about her travels. They were published for several weeks in the newspaper. With the assistance of donations, she helped with the education of a girl in Africa. She was invited by WBEN radio to share her life experiences on air. She spoke to many church and club groups and donations received from those talks went to her mission work in Assam, India, and Haiti, among other regions.

Mary was a Golden Heritage member of the NAACP and a life member of the YWCA. Her religious, volunteer, and community service activities awarded her numerous citations.

She was inducted by Gamma Phi Omega Chapter of Alpha Kappa Alpha Sorority, Inc. into the Black Hall of Fame in 1983.

She died on May 16, 1990.

Wanda Smith Hackney

Wanda Hackney is the wife of John Hackney, since 1954, and a mother of four extraordinary children, six grandchildren, and two great-grandchildren. She is an active member of the Trinity Baptist Church where she serves as a deaconess, usher, and Sunday school teacher. At Trinity, Wanda exercises her God-given talent in coordinating plays and various programs at the church for Christmas and Easter. The annual Chocolate Hour, associated with the celebration of Black History Month, was under her direction for more than ten years. Wanda is responsible for seeing that the church is decorated for events in addition to placing and arranging floral arrangements throughout the church. In 1997 Trinity Baptist Church named her *Woman of the Year*.

A graduate of Edward J. Meyer Memorial Hospital of Nursing in 1954, Wanda was the first African American who held the position of class president of the Student Union and Vice President of the class 1952-1954 at the University at Buffalo, The State University of New York. From 1954-1989, Wanda was a Registered Nurse at E.J. Meyer Memorial Hospital, now known as Erie County Medical Center. She served as a Preceptor for University at Buffalo students from 1980-1989. During her duration at Erie County Medical Center she was featured in a *Buffalo Sunday* editorial news story as an emergency room nurse (1979), and presented in a special television series called, *A Day with an Emergency Department Nurse* (1980). Later that year, Wanda was awarded the *Black Achiever's Award*. She served on the Board of Directors of an organization called WERMES - Wyoming Erie Regional Medical Emergency Service.

In 1989, Wanda was presented with a *Legislative Award of the Year* from the New York State Nurses Association and was recognized by Erie County Medical Center for outstanding contributions to the nursing profession. After thirty-five years of service with Erie County, Wanda Hackney retired. The Mayor of Buffalo, County of Erie, and the Buffalo Common Council presented her with a proclamation commending her prestigious career that was marked by dedication and diligence to patients, co-workers, and the community. After her retirement, she served for eight years as a Teen Life Educator/Nurse Educator for prenatal patients at Geneva B. Scruggs Community Center.

Wanda is a past member of the Coalition of 100 Black Women. She served on the Board of Directors for the Committee on Rape and Sexual Assault, Boys and Girls Scouts of America, District I Nurses Association, and Wyoming/Erie County Emergency Medical Services.

She is an avid world traveler - having traveled over twenty countries and most of the United States.

In 1997, Wanda was appointed coordinator of the World Day of Prayer Urban IV Cherry District. She has served in this capacity for five years and was saluted for years of dedicated service by Church Women United. Her family was selected as the *Family of the Year* sponsored by the Center for the Study and Stabilization of the Black Family at Niagara University (1998).

Wanda presently serves as President of the Afro-American Historical Association of the Niagara Frontier. She also served as past president of the Inter Club Council and was treasurer for eight years. She is past president of the Emergency Nurses Association, a Silver Life Member of the NAACP, a member of Erie County Medical Center Retirement Association, Church Woman United, and an active board member of Vision Quest Ministry.

Because of Wanda's upbringing she knew at an early age what she wanted to become. Her mother, Cozetta Smith, always taught her and her two older sisters that "nothing beats a failure, but a try." That is something that she has ingrained into her own children. From her extensive involvement, Wanda shows deep concern for the rights and dignity of human persons. She is compassionate and caring towards others. She has made a commitment in whatever she is involved with and serves as an excellent role model to girls and women of all ages. She is gentle, soft-spoken, and well versed in the facts of life. People respond well to her thoughtful and kind manner. She gives much of herself to others - thus most deserving to be designated as the Uncrowned Queen.

Dorothy Hill

Dorothy Elizabeth Hill is the first to note that as a mother of five, her primary achievement has been family centered. Her path of work experience from retail clerk at Berger's, to secretary at the International Institute, to her current position as President of the Langston Hughes Institute, have exemplified personal values and social responsibility.

Dorothy's professional career in community service began in 1965, when she fought with the Community Action Organization (CAO) in the war on poverty. She helped establish Buffalo's first Youth Opportunity Homes for troubled girls. After fifteen years as facility Director for three of these homes, she retired from the New York State Division for Youth. Still highly motivated by community needs and educational possibilities, she went back to work and created community-based projects such as Learning How to Learn About Africa seminars, and the *Reading Room* housed at the Humboldt YMCA. In addition, Dorothy was one of the founders of the Nile Valley Shule an African-centered private school. Also an entrepreneur, she became a merchant of fine fashions and fabrics.

Today, as the President and CEO of the Langston Hughes Institute, she has taken on the institution-building mission of revitalizing and developing this 32-year-old organization as a premiere art, cultural, and training center in Western New York.

Ora-Lee Khalid (Lewis-Delgado)

Ora-Lee was one of thirteen children (nine boys and four girls) born to William McQuiller and Essie Hogan in Port Huron, Michigan. She earned a business diploma from Lackawanna High School and an Associate's Degree in Small Business and Management Administration from Erie Community College in 1973. She also attended the University at Buffalo. In 1994, she was one of twenty-tree candidates in the United States who was selected to receive the Honorary Doctor of Laws Degree by the Board of Directors of Faith Grant College in Birmingham, Alabama.

In 1967, Ms. Delgado was hired as the Administrative Assistant to the Westminster Community House. In addition to her administrative duties, she often found herself working with many of the youth and young adults who attended the after school activities. She developed a positive relationship with young teens who often found themselves involved with gangs. In 1971, Lawrence, her 15-year-old son, was shot in a random shooting as he played baseball in front of their home. Ora-Lee addressed her pain and heartache by calming the gang members that rushed to her home. Many wanted to seek revenge for the death of her son.

That same year, *Mrs. D,* as she was now affectionately called, was offered an Administrative Assistant job at the Langston Hughes Institute where her duties would be all-encompassing. A Model Cities funded agency, the Institute lost that funding in 1973. Yet, Ora-Lee continued to volunteer her time for the next two years. In 1975, she was appointed Executive Director. The Institute's initial focus had been the visual and performing arts. Mrs. "D" expanded the program to include educational, technical, and industrial arts. Under her leadership, the Institute received funding from a number of sources. She retired from the Institute in 1996.

Ora-Lee serves on the American Association of Retired Persons (AARP) Congressional District Team; is a member and treasurer of the International League of Muslim Women; and volunteers for the American Cancer Society and the Grandmother's Program, tutoring students at St. John Christian Academy. She also is a part-time manager for Hope Lodge, a home for cancer patients and families in Buffalo.

Mrs. D is the recipient of numerous awards and honors including the *Citizenship Award*, Empire State Federation of Women's Clubs; *Service Award*, Phyllis Wheatley Club of Colored Women ; *Meritorious Service Award*, National Association of Negro Business and Professional Women's Clubs, Inc.; multiple Community Service awards from the Minority Management Association, Albany, New York; Buffalo Area Metropolitan Ministries; and Majid NuMan, Sister Clara Muhammad's University, Rochester, New York. Ora-Lee also has been nominated and approved by the New York International African Institute, Inc. and its International Advisory Board to receive the Institute's most sacred *African Ancestor's Award*. A posthumous award also will be given to her husband, Anthony "Tony" Delgado, better known as *Mr. D*, for his dedicated and sincere efforts to share the knowledge of African history.

In 1953, Ora-Lee accepted the teachings of Islam via her brother, Bobby McQuiller, a trainer for Muhammad Ali. After much research and many visits to libraries, she said many unanswered questions she had throughout her teenage years were finally answered. Elijah Muhammad appointed her Secretary in 1955. Her home and the home of her parents was the home-away-from-home for Minister Malcolm X during the establishment of a temple in the City of Buffalo.

Mrs. D has participated in many Islamic activities through Majid NuMan and other affiliated Masjids in the area. The many conventions and workshops provided numerous contacts throughout the country and from other Islamic countries. Her one desire is to make Hajj as soon as possible.

Ora-Lee continues to focus on two major issues: the covert and overt attempts to minimize the worth of African American organizations, and the struggles of African American youth to attain the American Dream. She says, "This file, in the table of my memory, will now be transferred in a book entitled *The Greatest Fight For Life*." The workshops that she and her late husband conducted at the East Ferry Erie County Youth Facility are the basis for this book.

She has completed the documentation of the workshop, *The Greatest Fight for Life*, and audiotape, and is in the process of putting this work on videotape to air on public access television. She also is working on public workshops that would be available to families throughout the Buffalo area. In addition, she is writing a book called *Memories In Time* that she hopes will serve as a legacy for her children, grandchildren, extended family members, and the general public. She believes that all of us have precious memories that should be shared as a "way of reaching out and touching other's lives."

Ora-Lee married Cornelius W. Lewis in 1950 and together they had seven children: Vincent Cornel (deceased), Andrea (Keith King), Craig (Marietta), Lawrence (deceased), Dawn (Bryant Perkins), T. Daynean, and Caroline Allahna. Her grandchildren are Kristin King, Taylor, Jennifer, Jordan, Austin Lewis, Lauren Lewis, and Lila Paige Perkins.

She married Tony Delgado in 1987 and he brought to the marriage daughters Maria (Andrew Tully), Madelaine Delgado-Massey, and Anthony Jr. (deceased), as well as grandchildren Eileen (Harold Bost), Michele (Michael Arnez), Madelaine (Eric), Louis Massey, Michael, Jeremy, and Antonia Arnez.

Ora-Lee's foremost desire is to continue, in her own way, to serve quietly and to affect individuals positively as she reaches out and touches any and all of humanity regardless of race, creed, color, or social status. Above all, she seeks to impact the lives of our youth – the future leaders of tomorrow.

Florence Lee

Florence Randolph Jackson was born in 1884 in Jersey City, New Jersey, and is the daughter of Charles Kersey Jackson and Mary Luvisa Bruce. She graduated from the Pratt Institute in Brooklyn, New York, around 1908, majoring in Fashion Design and Couture.

As a top graduate from the Pratt Institute, she was referred to work in Stearn's Department Store on 42nd Street, but when she went in for the interview, she was denied employment because of her color. After she left the store that day, she was walking along Fifth Avenue where she happened upon the salon of Madame Elaine Curtis, a French Couture shop. Florence asked to speak to the owner, showed her the portfolio she had brought for the Stearn's interview, and was immediately hired. Florence worked for Madame Curtis from 1908 - 1915 and she sewed for many executive wives living in the city.

In 1915, Florence married Edward David Lee and moved to Buffalo. Having spent so many years in New York City, she was well-versed in the arts and culture. Once she arrived in Buffalo, she quickly worked to introduce the literature and musical works of many black writers and composers to young black women.

She started the Lit-Mus Study Club in February 1922. Club members met monthly, usually in her home, at 69 Brooklyn Avenue (the house has since been torn down) and later at her home on Michigan Avenue. The club is still in existence and celebrated its 60th anniversary in 2002. The Lit-Mus hosted several prominent black artists to its meetings including Nathaniel Dett, James Weldon Johnson, and others. The Lit-Mus provided scholarships and awards to talented youth. Members did book reports and attended functions where prominent blacks were performing or speaking. The Lit-Mus Study Club initiated the first observance of Black History Month in 1928.

Eunice Lewin

Eunice Ashman was born on November 4, 1951, in Guantanamo, Cuba. She is the fourth of six children born to Washington and Lena Ashman. The family migrated to the United States in 1967. Eunice earned a Bachelor of Arts degree in Sociology from Marymount Manhattan College in New York City before moving to Buffalo in 1976. She obtained a Master's degree in American and Puerto Rican Studies in 1978, and a Master's degree in Educational Administration in 1989, both from the University at Buffalo.

Eunice volunteered at Buffalo Catholic Charities in 1976, before being employed there for three years as a Social Worker. She then obtained a position with the Erie County Department of Social Services in the Division of Child Protection. For the past twenty-one years, she has been employed as a Bilingual Social Worker for the Committee on Special Education at the Buffalo Board of Education. She is particularly concerned about our youth, the leaders of tomorrow, and about the downtrodden in our society.

Eunice has a passion for service and the sum total of her activities, past and present, reflects her deep commitment to our community. She serves on several Boards of Directors including Roswell Park Alliance, Founding Member Issues Committee and Speakers Bureau; Canisius College, Board of Regents, Trustee; Western New York Public Broadcasting Association, Trustee; The Buffalo Seminary; The Commission on the Status of Women, Commissioner; American Red Cross, Greater Buffalo Chapter, Hispanic Outreach Committee, Chair; Buffalo Urban League, Gala 2001 and 2002 Chair and Scholarship/Development Committee, Chair; Vestry, St. Philip's Episcopal Church, Endowment Committee, Chair; and the Niagara Frontier Transportation Authority, Commissioner. She also has held board positions with the Erie County Cultural Resource Advisory Board; YWCA of Western New York; Greater Buffalo Opera Company, Ball Chair (1992, 1993); Zoological Society Board; Buffalo Prep, Board Vice-Chair, Cotillion Chair (1998), and first graduating class Celebration of Achievement, Chair (1994, 1995); Roswell Park Alliance, Tree of Hope, Chair; All Star Night, Chair; *Herd About Buffalo*, Steering Committee; The Arts Council of Buffalo and Erie County, Nominating Committee; and the Clarkson Center, Courage to Come Back Awards, Selection Committee.

In addition, Eunice is a member of the Erie County Chapter of The Links, Incorporated and the Hispanic Women's League. In 1994, she was honored for her civic contributions at the Ebony and Ivory Ball. She also was inducted into The Western New York Women's Hall of Fame on March 14, 2002. The Women's Hall of Fame "honors those women in perpetuity who have worked in a public spotlight, as well as those who have quietly enriched the community and inspired others."

Eunice is married to Dr. A. Norman Lewin, a heart surgeon at Kaleida Health and a Director on its Board of Directors. They are the parents of two daughters, Elizabeth Maria and Eva Michelle.

Brenda McDuffie

Brenda W. McDuffie has been serving as President and CEO of the Buffalo Urban League, Inc. since October 1998. The Buffalo Urban League is committed to insuring that African Americans, minorities, and disadvantaged individuals have the opportunity to achieve their full potential. In her position with the Urban League, Mrs. McDuffie's energy and talent is dedicated to making real, positive changes in the lives of people in the Western New York community.

From 1994 to 1998, she was the Executive Director for the Buffalo and Erie County Private Industry Council, Inc. (PIC). In this capacity, she had the very challenging task of working with individuals and businesses to ensure that there was a high quality workforce to allow economic bases to grow. While at the PIC, Mrs. McDuffie served as President of the New York State Association of Employment and Training Professionals (NYATEP) where she also co-chaired and was a member of the steering committee. The committee produced the recommendations for New York State's future Workforce Development System.

She received her undergraduate degree from Buffalo State College, and earned a Graduate Certificate in Human Resource Development from the State University of New York at Buffalo, School of Management. Mrs. McDuffie started her career as a paralegal aide for Neighborhood Legal Services. She worked for the City of Buffalo Human Resources Department as Senior Manpower Coordinator and later served as Director of Planning at the Private Industry Council where she became Executive Director in 1994.

She currently serves on several Boards of Directors. She is immediate past President of Leadership Buffalo, Secretary for Independent Health Association, member of the Board of Directors for Western New York Foundation, Buffalo State College, the newly created Greater Buffalo Savings Bank, Buffalo Niagara Convention and Visitors Bureau, and is on the Trustee Council for Kaleida Health Systems.

She has received numerous awards and recognitions including *The Buffalo News Citizen of the Year*; the NAACP *Community Service* award; *Business First's Forty Under 40* award; and the United Way's *Volunteer of the Year*.

Mrs. McDuffie, her husband Gerald, and three children: Geralinda, Myllissa, and Gerald, reside in Buffalo. She and her family realize that all things are possible through God. They worship at the Elim Christian Fellowship.

Sandra Mobley-Terry

The Owner and President of Mobley-Terry and Associates Training and Program Development Consultants, Sandra Mobley-Terry is widely recognized for her expertise and for her dynamic and compelling training style. Her Competency Enrichment Training programs are used by both public and private organizations. She has developed curricula that promote empowerment through the appreciation of self and has been contracted by many agencies throughout the United States to facilitate workshops/seminars using that curricula as well as her Cultural Competency training module. Ms. Mobley-Terry's training modules, regarding Multicultural Awareness and Diversity Appreciation, Personal Enrichment, Team-Building, Conflict Resolution, Reducing the Risk of Violence in the Workplace, Customer Service, Sexual Harassment and Professional Enhancement and Empowerment, are tailored to the specific needs of the client.

Lake Shore Behavioral Health, Inc. employs Sandra as Director of their Residential Substance Abuse Treatment Facility for women with children. She is the past Director of the Erie County Committee on Rape and Sexual Assault, Inc., Founder and Past Director of the Training Institute for the Prevention of Violence against Women, and a former Director of the City of Buffalo's Division of Substance Abuse Treatment Services. In 1998, she inaugurated the agency, Survivors Break the Silence, Inc., which provides training focused on the impact of sexual violence to survivors.

Ms. Mobley-Terry is a past member of the boards of New York State Coalition Against Sexual Assault, Just Buffalo Literary Center, the Erie County Cultural Arts Resources Advisory Board, and the Buffalo and Erie County Historical Society. She is a past appointee to the Erie County Commission on the Status of Women.

Sandra currently serves on the executive board of the Niagara Frontier Council of the Boy Scouts of America and chairs the City of Buffalo's Commission on Citizens Rights and Community Relations.

A mentor and advisor to individuals and organizations throughout the Greater Buffalo and Western New York area, Sandra is the 1998 recipient of the *Planned Parenthood Award for Women's Health Advocacy*, the recipient of the National Conference for Community Justice's *Health Award*, and a graduate of Leadership Buffalo (1999).

Edith Robinson

After graduating Magna Cum Laude from Wilberforce University, Wilberforce, Ohio, Ms. Robinson embarked upon a career in social work administration, combined with volunteerism.

In her professional life, she worked for thirty-three years at the Erie County Department of Social Services (1947 to 1981). In rapid succession, her job responsibilities began as caseworker, unit supervisor, district supervisor, Assistant Deputy Commissioner, and concluded with her title of Deputy Commissioner of Social Services. During these years she had sole responsibility of Child Welfare, Medicaid, and Food Stamps for Erie County, as well as ancillary services for the entire department, i.e., accounting, message center, record room, staff development, etc.

In her administrative capacities, the Social Services Commissioner appointed her to membership in community services, e.g., the Greater Buffalo American Red Cross, the Community Action Organization, and United Way. She has been devoted to service in more than forty agencies.

Ms. Robinson has a legacy of having broken numerous racial and gender barriers. She adds many firsts to her credit: first black female Assistant Deputy Commissioner – Erie County Social Services; first black President of the American Lung Association of Western New York; first black local chairwoman of Volunteers, Vice Chairwoman Greater Buffalo, Chapter of American Red Cross; first black Vice Chairman and Secretary of the National Red Cross Convention; first black Chairwoman of the Eastern Area of National Red Cross (included Eastern Seaboard and Puerto Rico); first black Vice President of the Buffalo Chapter of the National Association of Social Workers; first black Vice President and President Elect of Zonta Club of Buffalo; first black Female Board Member of Buffalo Philharmonic Society; first black Board Member of Samaritan Counseling Center; first black President and Board Member of Bry-Lin Hospitals; first black Band Member of Interima Home Health Care; first black Chair of Admissions Committee of United Way of Buffalo and Erie County; and first black Professional volunteer to receive Certified Volunteer Administrator (CVA) in the United States.

Edith has been married for fifty-five years to James C. Robinson. They share a love of the same professional careers as well as a love of volunteerism. Their son, Wesley, is a retired parole officer and undercover agent for the Drug Enforcement Agency (DEA).

She is a Golden Soror (fifty years-plus membership) of Alpha Kappa Alpha Sorority, Inc. And she is active in Xi Epsilon Omega Chapter of the sorority.

Madeline O. Easley Scott

Madeline Scott is a native of Olean, New York, who moved to Buffalo in 1958. She is the daughter of Mrs. Lois Easley, another Uncrowned Queen.

Mrs. Scott is a graduate of Empire State College and has a Bachelor of Science Degree in Community and Human Services from that institution. She was selected in 1997 as one of Empire State College's Distinguished Alumni and is listed in *Who's Who in American Universities and Colleges*.

In 1990, she retired from Roswell Park Cancer Institute after a career that spanned thirty-two years.

She has been an active member of the Buffalo Community since her move here over forty years ago. She is a Golden Heritage Member of the NAACP and is active in the Buffalo Chapter as the Secretary and Membership Chair. As an Executive Board member since 1967, she has served on a number of local, regional, and statewide committees. She served four years as Membership Chair of the New York Branches and as second Vice President of the New York State Conference of Branches. Among her duties as Vice President was visiting and working with seven inmate NAACP Branches located in correctional facilities throughout the state. She has been active in the NAACP ACT-SO Program since 1978, serving as Secretary/Treasurer and recruiter of judges.

She also has been an active member of the Afro-American Historical Association of the Niagara Frontier since 1977. She has served as the President; Co-Editor of the newsletter, *Historically Speaking*; and is the founder and chair of the Association's Annual Family History Dinner.

Mrs. Scott is the recipient of numerous local and statewide civic, community, and organization awards, such as Buffalo Branch NAACP *Medgar Evers Civil Rights Award*, Black Achievers, *New Hope Baptist Church Martin Luther King Award*, and others. She is a member of St. Luke AME Zion Church, and is Chair of the Church Endowment Fund, and member of the Church Van Committee.

She is an avid genealogist and has researched different segments of her family back to slavery, as well as free members dating back to 1777. She is a member of the International Society of Sons and Daughters of Slave Ancestry. She conducts family history workshops for groups and individuals and at Oral History Conferences.

Mrs. Scott has authored two articles, "Proceedings of, and address delivered at the Colored Voters League Annual Meeting, Olean, New York, August 13-15, 1895" in the July 2000 edition of *Afro-Americans in New York Life and History*; and "Family History" in the 1977 issue of the same journal. In 1998, Mrs. Scott, and other family members, participated in the unveiling ceremonies of a monument in Washington, D.C., that honored 240,000 blacks who fought in the Civil War. Three of her ancestors, who served in the United States Colored Troops from New York, Ohio, and Michigan, are listed on the wall.

Mrs. Scott is a member of Alpha Kappa Alpha Sorority, Inc., Gamma Phi Omega Chapter and the Erie County Chapter of The Links, Incorporated.

Geneva B. Scruggs

Geneva Ellen Byrd Scruggs was born in Winfall, Virginia on June 11, 1906. She was the second of three daughters of Lee Faulkner Byrd, a Baptist Minister and Wilhelmina Scott Byrd, a public school teacher. Her early years were spent in Winfall and Lynchburg, where she attended elementary and high school.

As a student of St. Paul's Normal and Industrial School (St. Paul's College) she prepared for a career in elementary education. While there, she was active in many campus activities. Among those were president, campus YWCA; member of the debate team; Inter-Collegiate Orators Guild; and Inter-Collegiate Conference on World Affairs. She graduated valedictorian of her class with a medal of honor for excellence in English.

After teaching fifth grade at Campbell County Training School (Rustburg, Virginia), she visited relatives in Niagara Falls in 1932.

There she met and later married Leonard A. Scruggs, a local mortician. For six-and-a-half years they resided in Niagara Falls. Upon arriving in Buffalo, Mrs. Scruggs became involved in Republican politics. She served as an Inspector of Elections, District Committeewoman, and Vice-Chairman of the Fifth Ward. She also served as secretary of the New York State Republican Convention for two sessions; appeared on panels with Governor Thomas E. Dewey and Secretary Dulles. She was a candidate for Fifth Ward supervisor in 1955.

Mrs. Scruggs was a co-founder and first president of the School #75 PTA. She was awarded a gold pin for twenty-five years in scouting in 1965. For thirteen years, she served as Recreation Instructor at St. Mary's Parochial School and as Girls' Group Worker at Westminster Community House. She was the first director of the JFK Community Center. For seventeen years, she conducted a tax consultant service.

In 1950, Mrs. Scruggs was confirmed as a member of St. Philip's Episcopal Church. She had been continually active and served in many capacities as Church School Teacher, member of the Episcopal Church Women, and The Acolyte Mother's Guild (president, secretary and treasurer). In 1968, she was the first woman elected to the Vestry at St. Philip's, and served on the Board of St. Philip's Community Center. She served on the Budget and Finance Committees, as Church Fiscal Officer, member of the Stewardship Committee, and as member of the Christian Education Committee. At the Diocesan level, she served on the Committee for Restructuring the Diocese, Secretary of the Central Erie Deanery, Episcopal Charities Speakers Bureau, Consultant and Group Leader at the DeVeaux Conference, Member of the Standing Committee, and member of the Commission on Ministry and Society of the Companion of the Holy Cross, a nationwide organization following the Ministry of Intercession and Thanksgiving.

From 1967 until she retired in 1974, Mrs. Scruggs served as Director of St. Philip's Community Center. Among other boards on which she served are Council of Churches; St. Augustine's Community Center; United Way; 4-H of Erie County; Westminster Community House; Community Music School; Council to the Office for the Aging; National Conference of Christians and Jews; and Advisory Committee to the Board of Education.

Mrs. Scruggs was a founding member of Beta Phi Chapter, Iota Phi Lambda Sorority; Past Matron, Paramount Chapter #57, Order of Eastern Star (PHA); and Bison Assembly No. 48, Order of the Golden Circle.

Among her many citations are: Mother of the Year; Bishop's Cross; Woman of the Year; *Brotherhood Award*; *Community Award*; *Citizens Award*; *Outstanding Church Woman*; *Community Service Award*; *Outstanding Achievement Award*; *Distinguished Service Award*; and in 1979, she received the *Evans-Young Award* from the Buffalo Urban League.

Mrs. Scruggs is survived by four children: Yvonne Scruggs Leftwich, Leonard A. Jr., Harriet S. Lewis, and Roslyn S. Foreman, and seven grandchildren.

Mary B. Talbert

Mary Morris Burnett was born in 1866 and educated at Oberlin College. Following her graduation in 1886 from Oberlin, Ms. Burnett moved to Little Rock, Arkansas, where she accepted a position as a high school teacher. According to her biographer, Lillian S. Williams, Ph.D., Ms. Burnett taught history, math, science, Latin and geography at Bethel University before being appointed the school's Assistant Principal. Ms. Williams noted, "She was the only woman ever to be selected for this position."[2] In 1887, Mary Burnett was named principal of Union High School in Little Rock. While her abilities and talents as an educator and orator were recognized nationally as well as in Little Rock, according to the custom of the time, Ms. Burnett was forced to give up her teaching career once she married. Her marriage to William Herbert Talbert, a City of Buffalo clerk and realtor, took place on September 8, 1891.[3] The Talbert's only daughter, Sarah May, was born in 1892.

---

[2] Williams, Lillian S., "Mary Morris Burnett Talbert" in Hine, Darlene Clark, Elsa Barkley Brown, Rosalyn Terborg-Penn, Eds. *Black Women in America: An Historical Encyclopedia*. Brooklyn, New York, Carlson Publishers, 1993. p. 1137.
[3] Ibid.

Mary Talbert soon settled into the communal life of her new home. She joined her husband as a member of the Michigan Avenue Baptist Church and quickly began to organize educational and cultural programs for church and community members alike. She was the president of the church's Christian Cultural Congress, the vehicle for many cultural and educational activities. While many of the programs were organized for the education and development of black women, Mrs. Talbert did not limit her activities to the church. In 1899, she became one of the founding members of the Phyllis Wheatley Club of Colored Women. This remarkable group of women, the city's first affiliate of the National Association of Colored Women's Clubs, set an ambitious program of service to others in order to achieve the NACW mission and emulate the Club motto, *Lifting as we climb.*

It is often noted in her biographies that Mary Talbert was the first black woman to receive a Ph.D. from the University at Buffalo. However, this fact has never been proven conclusively. According to Williams, the University did not offer Ph.D. degrees before 1930, but it did offer certificates that were called doctorates. It is possible that Mary Talbert could have received one of these doctorate certificates leading to the confusion over the actual credentials.[4]

In November 1900, Mary Talbert, along with other members of the Phyllis Wheatley Club of Colored Women, organized a protest rally at the Michigan Avenue Baptist Church. They called on the Board of Managers of the Pan American Exposition to include the Negro Exhibit, an exhibit that presented the achievements of blacks since Emancipation, in the upcoming Exposition. The group also advocated for the appointment of a colored commissioner. Mary Talbert was proposed as a most able and capable individual to represent the Negro community in this position.

Mary Talbert's advocacy for black women included her involvement in and leadership of several organizations, in addition to the Phyllis Wheatley Club of Colored Women. In 1905, she opened her home to Dr. W.E.B. Dubois, John Hope, Monroe Trotter, and others who founded and organized the Niagara Movement, forerunner of the National Association for the Advancement of Colored People. In 1911, she became a charter member of the Empire Federation of Women's Clubs, and the group's second president from

---

[4] Ibid.

1912-1916.[5] In 1916, she was elected President of the National Association of Colored Women's Clubs. She was elected to a second two-year term as President of that organization in 1918. During her tenure as NACW President, Mary Talbert was instrumental in the preservation and restoration of the Frederick Douglass Home in Anacostia.

During World War I, Mary Talbert was active in the war bond drives, personally soliciting thousands of dollars in Liberty Bonds. Further, she served as American Red Cross Nurse with the American Expeditionary Forces in France. She also served as a delegate to the International Council of Women in Christiania, Norway in 1920. She was a national and international public figure who was a sought after speaker for her lectures on race relations, anti-lynching and women's rights. Her tireless efforts on the behalf of African American people earned her the NAACP *Springarn Award*. Mary Burnett Talbert was the first black woman to be honored with this prestigious recognition.

Mary Talbert died in 1923. She is buried in Forest Lawn Cemetery and Garden Mausoleum.

Carolyn B. Thomas

Carolyn B. Thomas, a native Georgian, has been married to Eugene D. Thomas for fifty-two years and has been a Buffalo resident since 1952. She is a graduate of Georgia State College and the University at Buffalo, and has completed post-graduate study at UB in the Social Sciences.

Mrs. Thomas was employed at Friendship House in Lackawanna for eleven years; at Child and Family Service Reach-out Program for seven years; and at Westminster Community House for five years.

She has been a member of Bethel AME Church for over forty-four years. She has been a delegate to the AME General Conference Nine Quadrennials for thirty-six years and served on the powerful Episcopal Committee for twenty-four years. She founded and

---

[5] Ibid.

organized the first AME Missionary AREA Society in 1960 in Western New York and the entire connection AME church.

She is a long-standing member of Federated Women's Clubs and organized the So-Re-Lit Debs of the Federated Women's Clubs (Teen Club). Mrs. Thomas also organized the Mary B. Talbert Civic and Cultural Club in Buffalo on February 3, 1974. Through this endeavor she sought to perpetuate the memory of this towering pioneer who made the City of Buffalo her home for many years.

She considers her greatest achievement, in partnership with the Community Action Organization (CAO), to be the establishment of the Western New York Food Bank in 1980. This accomplishment occurred under her direction as President of the Board of Directors. Today, the Food Bank serves 97,000 people in four Western New York counties. Mrs. Thomas is now Chairperson Emeritus.

As a result of her work with the Food Bank, *The Buffalo News* recognized her as one of the *Citizens of the Year* in 1983. In addition, she was named *Buffalonian of the Year* (1990) by former Mayor James Griffin. She has received numerous other awards in recognition of her work including the *Sojourner Truth Award* by the National Association of Business and Professional Women (1970); *Spotlight on Women Award* by the Coalition of 100 Black Women (1985); *Community Service Award* by the NAACP (1985); *Volunteer Service Award* by the National Conference of Christians and Jews (1985); *Evans-Young Award* by the Buffalo Urban League (1988); the Queen of Bethel honor (1998) (her husband was honored as King of Bethel the following year); Inductee into the Western New York Women's Hall of Fame (1999); and named one of one hundred leaders in Western New York in the 20th Century (1999).

She is a member of Alpha Kappa Alpha Sorority, Inc., Gamma Phi Omega Chapter; the Lit-Mus Study Club; the National Federated Women's Club; and the Women's Missionary Society of Bethel AME Church.

Uncrowned Queens in Education

Florence Baugh

Mrs. Baugh is the former President of the Board of Education of the City of Buffalo and the current Director of Neighborhood Services, Community Action Organization of Erie County, New York. Highly active in community service, she has dedicated her life to helping Buffalo's poor and disadvantaged. She rose quickly through the ranks of the Community Action Organization, where she began as an aide and today heads the Neighborhood Services Department. Her experience there tempered her for the demanding position of the President of the Buffalo Board of Education, an office she held from May 1975 until December 1980. She was re-elected President in July 1983. Mrs. Baugh continued to serve as an at-large-member of the Board of Education until July 1989. She also served as board member of the Western New York Education Services Council; Sheehan Memorial Hospital Board of Directors; President of the New York State Conference of Large Cities Boards of Education; The Council of Great Cities School Boards; Western New York Art Institute; and the National Association for Community Development. She presently serves as Church Clerk, Chairman of the Board of Trustees, and Church Organist of Providence Baptist Church. She has chaired the Ellicott Houses Board of Directors since 1978, and was a member of the Board of Trustees of D'Youville College from 1980-1988.

In 1986, she was appointed by Governor Mario Cuomo to serve on the Fourth Judicial Screening Committee for New York State and served in this position until 1994. She has received numerous community service awards from such groups as the Buffalo Chapter of Negro Business and Professional Women; the Black Educators Association; the University at Buffalo, *Alumni Award*; the National Conference of Christians and Jews *Educational Award*; was named *Outstanding Citizen of the Year* by *The Buffalo News* (1975); and *Citizen of the Year* by the Buffalo Kiwanis Club (1976). She attended the Millard Fillmore College at the State University of New York at Buffalo, and has received an Honorary Degree of Doctor of Humane Letters from

Canisius College (May 1976), and from Medaille College (1985). She received the State University of New York Board of Regents, Medal of Excellence on February 22, 1984; the State University of New York, *Distinguished Citizen Award* (1986); and the New York State School Board Association, *Everett R. Dwyer Award* (October 1987).

In January 1995, Mayor Anthony M. Masiello appointed Mrs. Baugh to the Economic Development Zone Board of Directors. That same year, she completed training in *Community Presence* and *Managing A Network* at the Maxwell School of Citizenship and Public Affairs, at Syracuse University. She also received a certificate of completion as a Certified Housing Counselor from Howard University in Washington, D.C. The National Association of Community Action Agencies certified Mrs. Baugh as a Community Action Professional (CCAP) in September 1995. In February 1996, she was appointed a member of the Board of Trustees of Villa Maria College, and in May of that year was appointed to the Chase Manhattan Bank Community Advisory Board.

Her awards include: the Erie Community College *Ebony and Ivory Award* (January 1997). In February 1997, Mrs. Baugh was one of twelve women (six living and six deceased) named to the newly established Western New York Women's Hall of Fame. She was selected as one of ten representatives from Western New York to participate in the President's Summit held in Philadelphia in April 1997.

Mrs. Baugh's guide for living is the Holy Bible. Her personal desire is, "justly, to love mercy, and to walk humbly with God."

She is the mother of five children and grandmother of nine.

Bettye Blackman

Bettye McDaniel Blackman is a former Vice-President and Ferry District member of the Buffalo Board of Education. Throughout her career, Mrs. Blackman has diligently pursued the education of children.

She received a Bachelor of Arts degree in Business Administration from Howard University in 1947 and a Masters Degree from the State University of New York at Buffalo in 1960. She attended Canisius College in 1968 as a post-graduate student in counseling.

She first taught business courses at the William Penn Business Institute in Philadelphia. Coming to Buffalo in 1954, she began teaching business courses at East High School in February, 1956. Mrs. Blackman was the first African American, female secondary school teacher in the district. She became a school counselor in 1967, retiring in 1985. In 1989, she became a Headstart Evaluation Consultant with Health and Human Services, Administration for Children and Families; and in 1994, joined the staff of the Research Foundation of the State University of New York at Buffalo's Academic Talent Search as a counselor.

Mrs. Blackman served as a founder and secretary of the Buffalo Negro Scholarship Foundation. The Foundation, under the leadership of her late husband, Dr. George E. Blackman, presented its first scholarships in 1961, and continued over the years assisting more than five hundred students financially as well as educationally. Mrs. Blackman has served on numerous boards and committees including Treasurer of the New York State Council of Large City School Boards; Member, Advisory Minority Issues, New York State School Boards Association; New York State TasCommittee on Public School Choice; and the Niagara Frontier Transpork Force on the Teaching Profession; Board Association's Ad Hoc tation Authority, Board of Ethics. In addition she served on Lay Committees at Rosary Hill (Daemen College); Buffalo General Hospital, School of Nursing; and the Admissions Committee, the State University of New York at Buffalo, School of Dentistry.

Some of the many awards received by Mrs. Blackman include the *Education Award* (1989) from the National Conference of Christians and Jews; the *Citizen of the Year* (1989) award from *The Buffalo News*; the *Bridge Builders Historical Award* (1990) from Alpha Kappa Alpha Sorority, Inc.; a 1990 award from the National Committee for School Desegregation; and the *Outstanding Intercultural Relations Education Award* (1988) from Quality Integrated Education.

Her membership affiliations include the Buffalo Chapter of Girl Friends, Inc.; the Harriet Tubman 300s; Alpha Kappa Alpha Sorority, Inc.; and St. Philip's Episcopal Church.

Mary Chappelle

Mary Crosby Chappelle was born on March 12, 1905, in Milton, Florida. Her father, Tilman Crosby, died when she was very young. Her mother, Mariah, died in 1967 at the age of eighty-seven. Mrs. Chappelle is the third oldest of four children and she is the only surviving member of her family.

In 1919, Mrs. Chappelle and her family left Milton to live briefly in Dover, Ohio. Eventually, they settled in another part of Ohio. She graduated from high school with honors and enrolled in Clark College, a Methodist College in Atlanta, Georgia. In 1926, she graduated Magna Cum Laude with a degree in Liberal Arts. She later attended Gammon Theological Seminary for four years and received a certificate of recognition. Mrs. Chappelle also attended the Atlanta School of Social Work.

She moved to Buffalo in 1935. In order to get a teaching position in the school system, she had to take twenty hours of special education before she was allowed to teach. Mrs. Chappelle taught in many of the schools in the Buffalo School District. She taught at School #75 until her retirement in 1975. In addition to being a career teacher, she has been a lecturer, dramatist, poet, singer, and preacher. She was a columnist for the *Empire Star*, a local black newspaper, for almost twenty-five years.

Mrs. Chappelle has been a Federated Woman for many years, once belonging to all three clubs in Buffalo at the same time (Phyllis Wheatley Club of Colored Women, Lit-Mus Study Club, and the Mary B. Talbert Civic and Cultural Club). She is a founding member and was instrumental, along with Mrs. Carolyn B. Thomas, in establishing the Mary B. Talbert Club.

For her many years of community work she has been honored by several organizations including receipt of the *Edgar Meggan Award*.

Mrs. Chappelle was married to Clarence Chappelle, on April 22, 1957. He died in December 1959. Mrs. Chappelle remained active in church and the community for many years.

Ouida Clapp

Ouida H. Clapp, a graduate of Talladega College, Alabama, and Wayne State University in Detroit, Michigan, was Director of English Language Arts in the Buffalo Public Schools for seventeen years until her retirement in 1985. She began her career as a teacher of English in 1948.

A leader in her profession, she served many years as a Director of the National Council of Teachers of English and chaired some of that organization's most important committees. She was a Past President and Fellow of the New York State English Council and a charter member and Past President of the Buffalo Area English Teachers Association. She is author of numerous articles and publications, including grammar and literature textbooks that are used in schools nationwide.

After her marriage to Claude D. Clapp, who eventually became Deputy Superintendent of Buffalo Public Schools and Associate Superintendent in charge of Finance and Personnel, she moved from Detroit to Buffalo. She joined Bethel AME Church, where she taught Sunday school and sang in the choir. She served on numerous community boards and especially enjoyed her board work with the Educational Opportunity Center, NAACP's ACT-SO, the Trocaire College Board of Trustees, Restoration Seventy-Eight, and the Buffalo Inner City Ballet. She was a Past President of Gamma Phi Omega

Chapter of Alpha Kappa Alpha Sorority, Inc., and a member of Lincoln Memorial United Methodist Church.

Among Mrs. Clapp's awards are the New York State English Council's award for Outstanding Instructional Leader in the State, the Martin Luther King Day *Outstanding Educator Award*, the Martin Luther King Day *Rosa Parks Award*, the *Spotlight on Women Award* of the Coalition of 100 Black Women, the *Medgar Evers Award* of the NAACP, and the *Sojourner Truth Meritorious Service Award* of the Association of Negro and Professional Women's Clubs.

Mr. and Mrs. Clapp have three children and eight grandchildren. They are: Karen Graves, who served on the National Board of the Episcopal Church and headed toward the priesthood before she died in an automobile accident in 1989; Dr. Karla F. Holloway is Dean of Humanities and Social Sciences, and William R. Kenan Professor of English and Linguistics at Duke University; and Dr. Leslie Clapp is a pediatrician and founder of Main Pediatrics in Buffalo.

Mrs. Clapp was among the first black persons to teach in the senior high schools of Buffalo and the first black woman to become a director of a major department in the Buffalo Public Schools. As Director of English Language Arts she was responsible for curriculum development, assignment, supervision, and evaluation of English teachers, staff development, textbook selection, examination preparation, and the system's program of essay and speaking contests, debates, and dramatic presentations.

Mrs. Clapp was one of three persons in the nation nominated by the executive committee of the National Council of Teachers of English to the Presidency of the Council. She headed such important committees including the Committee on Classroom Practices in the Teaching of English, the Committee for Spring Institutes on Teaching Minority Literatures, the Committee on Publications for Students, and the Committee on American Literature and the American Multicultural Heritage.

In her role as co-author of Scott Foresman's widely used, highly respected grades six through twelve anthology of American literature, the *America Reads Series*, Mrs. Clapp contributed to the development of a leading junior and senior high school textbook series. It was a forerunner in presenting a significant and representative number of black and third-world writers and characters in appropriate contexts.

Then, as senior author of the *Holt English Series for Grades K-8*, she led a team of writers who worked from a keen awareness of the language needs of all students. Further, included among her numerous professional articles and publications are articles about the need for classroom literature by and about black people. For example, articles like "Why Color it White?" and "The Invisible Child," which she wrote as Contributing Language Arts Editor of the *Instructor Magazine*, address matters of literature and language especially pertinent to black children.

Mrs. Clapp died in November 2000. In addition to her family, many mourn the passing of this extraordinary woman.

Patricia E. Clark

Patricia Elaine Adderley was born in Pembroke, West Bermuda. In 1954, her mother and stepfather moved to the United States. She later traveled with her Air Force family to Japan where she graduated from Johnson High School in June 1960. The family moved to Plattsburgh Air Force Base where Pat graduated from the Our Lady of Victory Secretarial School.

Ms. Clark has encompassed a tremendous amount of strength, versatility, and independence - qualities instilled by her mother, Thelma Batts.

In 1961, Patricia married a native of Buffalo and traveled to France where her former husband served with the Air Force from 1961 through 1963. They are the parents of DeAnna Elaine, Devon Keith, and Jaye Allyn Clark. Patricia and her family are members of the Lutheran Church of Our Savior where she served on the Deacon Board (Secretary), Board for Christian Education, Scholarship Committee, and Memorial Fund Board of Directors (Chair).

After two years at the Bryant and Stratton Women in Business Institute, where Patricia gained an Associate Degree in Business Administration and Management, she enrolled in Medaille College's Business program. During this time, she was employed by Assemblyman Arthur O. Eve at the Urban Revitalization Task Force. Patricia was instrumental in the business training and educational advisement of a number of students from the Educational Opportunity Center, St. Augustine Center's Youth Enrichment Program, Erie Community College's Youth Internship Program, and the University at Buffalo's Applied Public Affairs Program.

In July 1986 after completing her Bachelor of Science Degree in Business Administration at Medaille College, Patricia was employed at the University at Buffalo as a college preparatory program student counselor. After a year and a half, she was promoted to Director of the Science and Technology Enrichment Program (STEP) and the Structured Educational Support Program (SESP), and later Associate Director for the Office for University Preparatory Program (OUPP) in September 1991. Ms. Clark has amassed twenty years of experience in budget management and counseling at the local and state level of public and private sectors. While employed by the University, Patricia completed a Master's Degree in Education.

Director Clark has received many awards for her services to the community including the Buffalo Engineering Awareness for Minorities (BEAM); Phi Beta Sigma Fraternity, Inc., *Social Action Award*; University at Buffalo, Chapter NSBE, *Honorary Member Award* and *Support and Dedication Award*; UB Upward Bound Program, *Personal Service Award*; and the Science and Technology Enrichment Program (STEP) Parents Association, *Outstanding Dedication and Years of Service Award*. Ms. Clark received corporate and national recognition in the May edition of the *National Society of Black Engineers Magazine* (Volume 6, Number 5) for "Selflessly participating in the endeavors of the society." In addition, the Buffalo Common Council proclaimed June 7, 1992, "Patricia E. Clark Day."

She served as an Internship Supervisor for Cora P. Maloney College's Community Services Internship Program; Instructor for ULC 101; a Certified Field Educator at the School of Social Work; and Grant Writer for the University at Buffalo. Ms. Clark was an outstanding guest speaker for numerous organizations. Some of her presentations include: *Deputy Speaker Speaks*, WBFO Radio and Channel 18 television; *STEP/CSTEP* at the New York State Education Budget Hearing, Leadership Conference; An Education Success Story, SUNY Institute of Technology-Symposium on Student Learning; SED Science and Technology Entry Program, Best Practices Conference, *Developing Successful Parent Advisory Groups*; UB's Minority Management Society; the Center for Academic Development

Services; and the STARS 96 Conference, *Students Technology Assessment Resulting in Success*. She also is a member of Delta Sigma Theta Sorority, Inc., Buffalo Alumnae Chapter.

Patricia's professional objectives are to be instrumental in educational administration, particularly in policy and program development, as well as implementation and analysis, and to have a significant impact on the education of minorities, women, and disadvantaged populations.

Rani Cox-Rawles

Rani Hale was born in Buffalo to George and Robuty Hale on November 9, 1927. She attended Elementary School #12 and graduated from Fosdick Masten Park High School. Rani was an exemplary student, a path she set to follow throughout her life.

At the age of twenty-one, she left Buffalo for Europe to attend the University of Paris at Sorbonne. Rani worked and received her Bachelor of Arts, Batchelor of Science, Master of Arts, and Master of Science degrees. She moved to New York City where she lived for several years before returning home to be with her mother. Rani continued her education at the University at Buffalo and completed her Ph.D. studies in 1965.

She was baptized into the Emmanuel Temple, Seventh-Day Adventist Church by Pastor Russell T. Wilson. She worked as a teacher in the Sabbath School Department, radio broadcast consultant, and consultant/advisor for the Education Committee.

Rani was a project administer for the Buffalo Board of Education from 1970 until her retirement. She taught English, among many other things, from 1957 to 1970 at then East High School. Her outreach was known in the education and civic circles. Some of her membership organizations included: the Black Educators Association, National Education Association, Future Teachers of America (Advisor), Project Able, Buffalo Psychiatric Center, Girl Scouts of America (Board of Directors), Society for the Prevention of Cruelty to Children, and the American Museum of Natural History.

Her other educational endeavors included positions as an instructor in Aspire; Director of the CAC Youth Employment; Commencement Speaker at Kleinhan's Music Hall; and Lecturer at the University of Bombay, India (1972). In addition, she was a community consultant for several local television news stations.

Rani married Cornelius Rawles on November 28, 1959. They were married for thirty-six years until her death on February 23, 1996.

Frances K. Hall

Frances K. Hall was born in Thomasville, Georgia, but has been a resident of Buffalo since infancy. She attended P.S. #75 and Hutchinson Central High School. She received a Bachelor of Arts degree from Talladega College in Talladega, Alabama, and a Bachelor of Science degree in Library Science from the University at Buffalo.

She was the first black trained librarian in the City of Buffalo. Mrs. Hall began her career at North Jefferson Branch Library. She later became a Field Worker with the Buffalo and Erie County Public Library. In this position, she traveled all over Erie County helping to upgrade town and city libraries. As a result of a recommendation submitted by Leeland Jones, Jr., a member of the Board of Supervisors, she and her fellow librarians helped to establish libraries at the Erie County Home and Infirmary, Erie County Holding Center, and Erie County Penitentiary. She retired from the library system as Assistant Deputy Director of Personnel. The Professional Librarian's Association honored her as Librarian of the Year in 1973.

Mrs. Hall was one of the founding members of Gamma Phi Omega Chapter of Alpha Kappa Alpha Sorority, Inc. The chapter has grown from the original seven members to over 180 sorors.

She has served as a board member for the Buffalo Urban League, Legal Aid, and Coordinated Care Management Association. She has volunteered for the American Red Cross and American Lung Association. She is a member of Buffalo Chapter of The Links, Incorporated; Gamma Phi Omega Chapter of Alpha Kappa Sorority;

Harriet Tubman 300s; and a life member of the NAACP. In addition, she is a member of Lincoln Memorial United Methodist Church were she has served as a member of the Pastor Parish and Nominating Committees. She is a former member of the Zonta Club.

Mrs. Hall was married to the late Thomas B. Hall, Sr., and is the mother of two sons, Thomas B. Hall, Jr., and Glowver D. Hall. She has two grandchildren, Miles L. Hall and Allegra Bess Hall. Her sons and grandchildren reside in Seattle, Washington.

Thelma Hardiman

Thelma Ayers Hardiman, a native of Memphis, Tennessee, received her Bachelor of Arts degree from LeMoyne College in Memphis and a Master of Public Health degree from the University of Michigan. She has been a trailblazer in many of her accomplishments. She was one of the first African American females to receive a Master's degree in Public Health, which stemmed from her interest in tuberculosis because of a family member's affliction. She later received postgraduate credits from the University at Buffalo in Education. A retired educator, she was the first African American female assistant principal to be appointed as acting principal in the City of Buffalo, and was among the few African American school principals at the time of her appointment. She has been cited for her work with special students and for her innovative disciplinary methods that emphasized reward rather than punishment.

Mrs. Hardiman has distinguished herself in her career and in community service. Through her many volunteer activities and leadership positions, she has been a role model and mentor to many for more than fifty years. Because of her tireless efforts and empathy, her activities and accomplishments have often been directed at helping others.

As a member and former president of the Alpha Kappa Alpha Sorority, Inc., an international organization of over 150,000 women, she saw a need and introduced to this area the Debutantes program and Ball, an event for young African American women that provides them with cultural enrichment, training and grooming, self esteem, confidence, and prepares them for the adult world as they make their informal debut into society. Many teenagers have developed into productive young women as a result of their experience and participation in the program. The Debutante Ball has become a Buffalo community tradition.

In 1950, Mrs. Hardiman became a charter member of the then newly organized local chapter of The Links, Incorporated. Her role in this international organization of eleven thousand women is exceptional. She has twice been elected president of the Buffalo chapter, and has been the General Chairperson of the Chapter's annual Ebony Fashion Fair, which she introduced to the Buffalo area in 1958. For forty-one years, she chaired the event that has produced thousands of dollars in scholarship funds annually for high school seniors. She has provided leadership at the local, regional, and national levels in The Links, Incorporated serving as Eastern Area Director, National Chapter Establishment Officer, National Vice President, and various other offices and specialized roles that utilize her unique talents and strong dedication to service.

Mrs. Hardiman has served on many boards including Studio Arena Theater, Buffalo Arts Commission, Hallwalls, Health Systems Agency of Western New York, Inc., and the Young Women's Christian Association (YWCA) where she served as Board President. She was the first African American elected to serve as the President of a metropolitan YWCA.

In recognition of her service, Mrs. Hardiman has been the recipient of numerous awards and honors including the Buffalo Urban League *Family Award*; Health Systems Agency of Western New York, Inc., *Certificate of Service*; NAACP, *Rosa Parks Award*; Council of Churches, 1986 *Philip Melanchthon Award*; YWCA, *Woman of the Year*; City of Buffalo, *Community Good Neighbor Award*; Buffalo Youth Board, *Merit Award*; and the *National Sojourner Truth Meritorious Service Award*. Mrs. Hardiman appeared in the first edition of *Who's Who Among American Women*. Mayor Anthony M. Masiello proclaimed October 23, 1998, *Thelma Ayers Hardiman Day* in recognition of her "tireless efforts and much appreciated contributions to a very grateful community" as General Chairman of the Ebony Fashion Fair.

Her commitment to her church is as evident as her commitment to her community. She devotes much time to programs for youth and family. She was former Chair of the Board of Education for the Lutheran Church of Our Savior. She was the first woman elected President of a church council at Missouri Synod, Lutheran Church. In addition, she served as Chairperson for Mission Outreach at Lincoln Memorial United Methodist Church, She also is Chair of Volunteers for the Central City Café.

Mrs. Hardiman was married to the late Winton "Flash" Hardiman, and has one daughter, Dr. Joye Hardiman, and a granddaughter, Salmh, of Tacoma, Washington.

Cecelia B. Henderson

Cecelia Henderson is a native of Hampton Virginia. She is a graduate of the University at Buffalo where she received both an undergraduate and graduate degree. Her area of postgraduate studies was in Prevention, Crisis, and Substance Abuse.

For thirty-four years Mrs. Henderson worked as a Prevention Specialist for the Buffalo Board of Education. While in this capacity, she was a curriculum member responsible for drug and sex education; certified HIV/AIDS instructor; coordinator of the New York State Pilot Drug Program; committee member for teacher candidate interviews; curriculum resource facilitator; and health education teacher. Her professional memberships included the Student Assistance Personnel (SAP) program, Buffalo Teachers Federation, New York State Education Association, National Education Association, Student Assistance Professionals Organization, and the Retired Teachers Organization. Mrs. Henderson retired from her position with the Board of Education in 1999.

An active member of the New Hope Baptist Church, Mrs. Henderson serves as Secretary on both the Board of Christian Education and Budget Committee. She also chaired numerous church events including the 20th Pastoral Anniversary and Retirement; Dr. Martin Luther King, Jr., Commemorative Breakfast; Graduate

Recognition Banquet, Homecoming Celebration, Scholarship Committee; and Youth Enrichment Program.

Mrs. Henderson has been a very active member of The Links, Incorporated for nearly thirty years. She has served the organization on the local, regional, and national levels. She is a Life Member of Alpha Kappa Alpha Sorority, Inc. where she currently serves as the Great Lakes Region Program Chair. In addition, Mrs. Henderson is an active member in several civic organizations. These include H&G Family Club (past President), Nardin Academy Parent's Council (past President), American Lung Association of Western New York (Board Director), New York State Lung Association (Board Director-at-large), Buffalo Philharmonic Orchestra Society (Board Director), Afro-American Historical Society, NAACP ACT-SO, Buffalo Urban League, and American Association of University Women.

Mrs. Henderson has been the recipient of numerous awards in recognition of her service to the community: Buffalo Ambassador (2000); Network of Religious Communities, Outstanding Ecumenical Service (2000); Alpha Kappa Alpha Sorority, Inc., Gamma Phi Omega Chapter, *Service Award* (1999); *Award of Excellence*, Black Achievers in Industry (1998), 1490 Jefferson Enterprises; Buffalo Board of Education award, *Services to Youth* (1998); Alpha Kappa Alpha Sorority, Inc., *Service Appreciation Award*, Xi Epsilon Omega Chapter (1998); National Council of Negro Women, *National Community Leader of the Year* (1997); New York Council of Negro Women, New York State *Community Leader of the Year* (1997); Dr. Martin Luther King, Jr. *Helping Somebody Award* (1997); Citizens Committee on Rape, Sexual Assault, Sexual Abuse, *Excellence in Leadership Award* (1996); Police Community Services, *D.A.R.E. Award* (1996); *Who's Who Among American Educators* (1996); Buffalo Teachers Federation, *Outstanding Dedication and Commitment Award* (1995); American Lung Association of Western New York (1994); Buffalo Ambassador (1991); Outstanding Alpha Kappa Alpha Sorority, Inc. Soror (1984); and Outstanding Young Women of America (1973).

Mrs. Henderson is married to Dr. Leon Henderson, Director of Personnel (Retired), Buffalo Board of Education. They have three children, Celia F. Settles, Leon Henderson, Jr., and Tanya E. Henderson, and four grandchildren.

Sharon Jordan Holley

Sharon Jordan Holley hails from High Springs, Florida. She now makes her home in Buffalo with her husband Kenneth and their three daughters. She is a graduate of Santa Fe Community College in Gainesville, Florida. She also is a 1970 graduate of Florida Atlantic University in Boca Raton, earning a Bachelor of Arts degree in English/Education. In 1972, she received a Master of Science degree in Library Science from Wayne State University in Detroit, Michigan.

Sharon has been employed as a Librarian with the Buffalo and Erie County Public Library since 1972. Her current position as Coordinator of Urban Services in the Department of Extension Services includes supervision of Buffalo's fifteen city branches and outreach activities in Urban Services. Prior to this position, she served as Head of the Children's Department of the Central Library, Branch Manager in several of the city branch libraries, and as an Assistant Librarian. Sharon holds membership in the Black Caucus of the American Library Association and works locally with the African American Librarians of Western New York.

Her gift of storytelling has led to many opportunities. She is a founding member of Spin-A-Story Tellers of Western New York, Co-coordinator of Tradition Keepers: Black Storytellers of Western New York, and performs as *We All Storytellers* with Karima Amin. Sharon served on the Board of the National Association of Black Storytellers, Inc. where she is still a member and has been a featured teller and workshop presenter at the national festival. She also has been a member of the National Storytelling Network. Her storytelling piece: "African American History Rap" was published in *Talk that Talk: An Anthology of Black Storytelling*, edited by Linda Goss and Marian Barnes (Simon and Schuster, 1989) and in *The African American Book of Values*, edited by Steven Barboza (Doubleday, 1998). A story from her repertoire, "Stagecoach Mary" was published in *Many Voices: True Tales from America's Past* (National Storytelling Press, 1995). Sharon has presented storytelling programs and workshops throughout Western New York and other places in the United States.

As a student of history, Sharon serves on the Board and as past President of the Afro-American Historical Association of the Niagara Frontier. She works with the Association to chair the annual Carter G. Woodson Essay Contest, co-edit the newsletter *Historically Speaking*, and serves on the Committee for the African American Ancestral Heritage Tour. She has served as the convener for the Coalition of African and African American Historical Groups where she directed the first African American Historical Brochure for Western New York. In 1999, she was appointed to serve as a Commissioner for the New York State Freedom Trail.

Sharon and her husband, Kenneth, owned and operated Harambee Books and Crafts in the City of Buffalo for twenty-one years. In addition to having a well-stocked store of books and materials by and about people of African descent, the store was a cultural meeting place for African American authors and resources in the community. Sharon and Kenneth were co-coordinators of the Buffalo Kwanzaa Committee, planning citywide celebrations of the African American Holiday of Kwanzaa for twenty-one years. The bookstore also was an organizing stop for African American study groups and citywide Malcolm X and Marcus Garvey celebrations.

Sharon also is a member of the Buffalo Genealogical Society of the African Diaspora and Advisory Committee of the Monroe Fordham Regional History Center at Buffalo State College. She works with numerous organizations, such as Juneteenth of Buffalo, Inc., Buffalo Quarters Historical Society, and the Association for the Study of Classical African Civilizations. She has received numerous awards and recognition for her service to the community. For this she gives thanks to God for the nurturing guidance of her parents, the late Johnnie and Rebecca Jordan of High Springs, Florida.

Muriel Howard

Muriel A. Howard, Ph.D., is the first female president of Buffalo State College and the seventh president in the school's history. She received her Doctorate (Educational Organization, Administration and Policy) and Master of Education degrees from the University at Buffalo, the State University of New York. She was the first female vice president at the University at Buffalo, serving as the vice president for Public Service and Urban Affairs.

Dr. Howard served as the first African American female chair of the United Way campaign for Buffalo and Erie County in 1999. She has served on numerous boards including the Erie County Executive's transition team, Studio Arena Theater, Fleet Bank, and the Buffalo Museum of Science. She also chaired the subcommittee on Youth Services and Education.

She has received numerous awards for her contributions in education and services to the community. Among some of the most recent are the *Governor's State Division of Women Award for Excellence in Education*, the *American Jewish Committee Institute of Human Relations Award*, the University at Buffalo's *Distinguished Alumni Award*, the Minority Bar Association of Western New York *Award for Community Service*, the Black Educators Association of Western New York's *Educator of the Year* award, and numerous others. She is the recipient of the State University of New York *Chancellor's Award for Excellence in Professional Service*, and was a charter inductee into the Western New York Women's Hall of Fame.

Dr. Howard is a member of Delta Sigma Theta Sorority, Inc., Buffalo Alumnae Chapter and the Erie County Chapter of The Links, Incorporated.

Donna S. Rice

Donna S. Rice currently serves as Associate Vice President for Student Affairs at the University at Buffalo. She holds both Bachelor and Master of Arts degrees in Linguistics, and a Ph.D. in Communications from the University at Buffalo. Dr. Rice has held numerous teaching and administrative positions at UB since 1972.

For more than 15 years she fulfilled several roles in the University's English Language Institute, first serving as an instructor of English as a Second Language, and later as Coordinator of Grammar, and Assistant Director for English Credit Programs. She was then named Assistant Director for Intensive English Programs and continued in that role until 1985.

In 1981, her strong interest in international education led her to accept an appointment in Beijing, the People's Republic of China, where she served as Director-in-Residence for UB's English Language Training Center. Dr. Rice was the first African American invited to teach English in Beijing. She continues to serve on the Council of International Studies and Programs at UB. She is a Citizen Ambassador for the *People to People Ambassador Program* and was invited to join the Women in Society Delegation to Egypt in October 2000.

Dr. Rice also served UB as Staff Associate in the Office of the President, under former President Stephen B. Sample; Director of the Educational Opportunity Program (EOP); and Associate Vice President for Special Programs. Current University roles include Chair of the Committee for the Promotion of Respect for Diversity; Treasurer of Phi Beta Kappa, Omnicron Chapter; and Chair of the Affirmative Action Committee for the Professional Staff Senate.

She has held numerous national, state, and local offices in various professional organizations. At the national level, she has served as At-Large-Representative to the National Association for Foreign Student Affairs (NAFSA); Coordinator for the NEEED Mentoring Network of the National Association for Student Personnel Administrators (NASPA); Chair of the Diversity Committee of the American

Association of University Administrators (AAUA) and several terms on the AAUA Board of Directors. Currently, she sits on the National Diversity Advisory Council of the American Red Cross.

Locally, Dr. Rice has contributed over the years to numerous community organizations and committees including tenure as a Democratic Committeewoman for the former 16th District; President of School 57 PTA; membership on the Geneva B. Scruggs Health Center and Neighborhood Information Center (NIC) Boards of Directors; Vice Chair and Treasurer of the Bethel Head Start Policy Committee; United Way Day of Caring Team Leader; American Red Cross Donor Services Advisory Committee, Buffalo Chapter; and Past Secretary of the Board of Directors of Leadership Buffalo.

She currently serves on the Board of Directors of the New York/ Penn Region of the American Red Cross; Board of Directors of the National Council for Community and Justice (NCCJ); and Board of Directors of the King Urban Life Center. Children are her passion and she also continues to serve as President of the Board of Trustees of the King Center Charter School, Buffalo's first Charter School.

Dr. Rice has been the recipient of several awards for achievement and community service over the years. She was elected to Phi Beta Kappa and Alpha Lambda Delta honor societies, and also was named a Black Achiever in Industry by 1490 Jefferson Enterprises. She was later elected to the Leadership Buffalo Class of '89, and cited for Outstanding Community Service by the Erie County Executive in 1990. In 2000, she was cited in the *Year 2000 Millennium Edition of Who's Who Among Women,* and also invited to join the People to People Ambassador Program's Women in Society Delegation to Egypt. In 2001, she was the recipient of the NCCJ Education Award at the 48th Annual NCCJ Brotherhood/Sisterhood Awards Luncheon, and the University at Buffalo Campus Ministries' *Didaskalos Award.*

Dr. Rice truly believes in the notion of "lifting as we climb" and has been a Youth Sponsor for the William-Emslie YMCA for several years. She is a mother of three adult children and has been an active member of Humboldt Parkway Baptist Church, formerly the historic Michigan Avenue Baptist Church, for more than fifty years. She also is a member of Delta Sigma Theta Sorority, Inc., Buffalo Alumnae Chapter, and a Life-time Member of the NAACP and Partners of America.

Mrs. Albert Thompson

Mrs. Albert Thompson was the first black teacher in Buffalo. She taught in a segregated black school in old Vine Alley before the turn of the century. Vine Alley was eliminated in the Ellicott redevelopment in the area near Emergency Hospital. The school was torn down in the early 1900s.

Sherryl D. Weems

Dr. Sherryl D. Weems has been the Director of the University at Buffalo, Educational Opportunity Center for over ten years. She came to Buffalo from New York City and received a Bachelor of Science degree in Elementary Education with a concentration in Spanish from SUNY College at Fredonia. Dr. Weems received both a Master's degree and Doctorate in Education from the University at Buffalo. She also is a graduate of the Management Development Program at Harvard University.

Despite her heavy work schedule, she is an original founding Board member of Buffalo Prep and still serves on the Advisory Board. She also is on the Board of Directors of the Arts in Education Institute of Western New York. Her other volunteer activities include the Urban Education Institute Policy Board and the IQ Task Force at the University at Buffalo. Dr. Weems is a member of Leadership Buffalo and the Rotary Club of Buffalo. She is a former board member of the YWCA and the Advisory Board of the Salvation Army.

Her experiences are not limited to the academy. She devotes much of her time and energy to community development projects and research activities that focus on youth, workforce development, issues of diversity, and organizational dynamics. Dr. Weems has numerous community commitments including membership on the Board of Directors of Goodwill, Inc.; the Erie/Niagara Tobacco Free Coalition; and was appointed to the New York State Workforce Investment Board.

Dr. Weems also has received numerous awards of appreciation and recognition including the Rev. Martin Luther King Human Relations Award for SCLC and the Distinguished Alumnus Award from the State University of New York Office of Special Programs. Other organizations from which she has received awards include recognition from the Centennial AME Zion Church, the Community Action Organization (CAO), and the Masjid Numan-Clara Mohammed School for her commitment to youth and children. She also is very active with her boys in many sports and is coach for her son's basketball team. Dr. Weems is a member of Elim Christian Fellowship Church.

Uncrowned Queens in Health

Georgia Mackie Burnette

Georgia Mackie Burnette was born and raised in Buffalo. She graduated from P.S. #32 and Fosdick Masten Park High School.

In the 1940s, with the exception of the former E.J. Meyer Memorial Hospital (now Erie County Medical Center), Buffalo hospitals did not accept black nursing students. When her application to E.J. Meyer was rejected, she discovered that being married also carried a penalty. Nevertheless, Lincoln School for Nurses, Bronx, New York - an all-black school - accepted her as a student. After six months she returned home after learning that a nursing program awarding a Bachelor of Science degree was being offered at the University at Buffalo. She graduated in 1955, as one of the first black students in the nursing program. She continued her education and obtained a Master of Science degree in Nursing from the State University of New York at Buffalo, and a Master in Education from Niagara University. She continues to audit courses in areas of interest at local institutions of higher learning.

From 1960 through 1965, she was employed as Instructor of Nursing at Cook County School of Nursing and Provident Hospital School of Nursing, an all-black facility, in Chicago, Illinois. She later returned to Buffalo and was appointed to leadership positions at prominent healthcare facilities in Western New York, including Associate Director of Nursing, Buffalo General Hospital; Assistant Professor of Nursing, Niagara University; Director of Nursing, Roswell Park Cancer Institute; and Director of Nurses, Buffalo Psychiatric Center. In each instance, excluding Roswell Park, Mrs. Burnette was the first black nurse in the position.

Her community involvement activities include BUILD of Buffalo where she was active on the Education committee. She also was a board member of the former Family Service Society of Buffalo, now Child and Family Services. As a result of this experience, she was appointed Board Chairperson of the Reach out Program that assisted inner city residents with housing, health, and educational issues. Mrs. Burnette was a six-year member of The Grace Manor Board of

Directors; returning after a two-year hiatus for an additional year following the opening of the nursing home. Three years of service on the board of Restoration Society Clubhouses ended in May 2001. Mrs. Burnette is a member of the Buffalo Genealogical Society of the African Diaspora.

In the professional community, Mrs. Burnette served on the board of the Surgical Technology Advisory Committee of Niagara Community College. To date, she is the only black nurse to have served as President-Elect and President of the Professional Nurses Association of Western New York, District I, New York State Nurses Association. She also served as a board member of Nurses House, an organization assisting nurses in need throughout the United States.

Mrs. Burnette continues her membership in the Professional Nurses Association, District I, New York State Nurses Association. She is a member of the Afro-American Historical Association of the Niagara Frontier and the Advisory Board of the African American Family Reunions and Philanthropy, Philadelphia, Pennsylvania. She is a lifetime member of the NAACP and the Alumni Association of the State University of New York at Buffalo.

She is a recipient of the Mary B. Talbert Civic and Cultural Club award for *Outstanding Contributions to the Buffalo Community*; New York State Department of Health, *Outstanding Service Certificate for Work on the Inter-Agency Task Force on Women's Issues*; and the *Ruth T. McGrorey Award* for contributions to the Advancement of Nursing, presented by the Professional Nurses Association of Western New York, District I, New York State Nurses Association.

Mrs. Burnette has articles published in *Supervisor Nurse* (now *Nursing Administration*), *Reunions Magazine*, and the *Amherst Bee*. She launched the healthcare column for the *Buffalo Gazette*, and currently writes "Focus on Health" for the *Buffalo Criterion*.

Since retirement in 1993, Mrs. Burnette has explored interests in a variety of settings. She initiated the Health Education program for seniors at the William-Emslie YMCA, and was honored by that facility for her work.

Mrs. Burnette became interested in reunion planning when she and her husband, Luther, coordinated the Burnette family reunions in 1997 and 1999. She was the force behind the formation of the Burnette Family Association which assists family members in the areas of health, education, and economics. She is the editor of *The Burnette*

Bugle, the family newsletter. Mrs. Burnette is a frequent speaker at the African American Family Reunion Conference, Philadelphia, Pennsylvania. She recently held a reunion of the remaining members of the Webelows, a male group of friends formed in the late 1930s at the Chapel. The history of the club will be submitted to the Afro-American Historical Association of the Niagara Frontier.

Mrs. Burnette audited courses in the School of Journalism during the 2000-2001 fall and spring semesters at Buffalo State College and is a "wannabe" writer in the area of magazine and feature writing. She pursues that goal as time permits.

She firmly believes that for black Americans, education must be viewed not only as an approach to employment, but more importantly, as the way to expand one's view of the world and greater enjoyment of life.

Dr. Leslie E. Clapp

Dr. Leslie E. Clapp, a Board Certified physician and clinical associate professor of pediatrics at the University at Buffalo, is a graduate of Buffalo Public Schools, Oberlin College, and the University of Cincinnati, School of Medicine.

A founding member of the Buffalo Chapter of the National Medical Alliance, she initiated its mentor program for minority medical students, linking them to established local African American physicians. A fellow of the American Academy of Pediatrics, she also is a member of the Buffalo Pediatric Society and the Erie County Medical Society. She serves on the Board of Directors of the United Way, the Children's Hospital Residency Recruitment and Admissions Board, and the Medical Management Board of Community Blue.

Founder of Main Pediatrics, Dr. Clapp enjoys speaking to young people who seek her advice in civic, church, school, and other organizational settings, as well as encouraging her young patients to engage in good physical and mental health habits and to strive towards excellence in their career goals. She knows she is fortunate to have achieved many of her own personal aspirations. This strengthens her commitment to serve others. She values education, believing it is vital to the success of efforts to improve the socioeconomic condition of African Americans. Dr. Clapp feels keenly the need for more black physicians in Buffalo and actively seeks to help to this end, she has worked on the University's College of Medicine Admissions Committee.

Dr. Clapp's counsel, sought by mothers, grandmothers, aunts, sisters, and friends of her patients, is caring and highly valued. Her honest, concerned approach encourages acceptance, and many women in the community attribute much needed assistance and relief from pressure to her.

Many organizations in the area have paid special honor to Dr. Clapp. She is recipient of the Agape African Methodist Episcopal Church's *Women's Day Award*; the Student National Medical Alliance's *Award for Outstanding Contribution to Minority Medical Students*; the *Community Service Award* of the African American Police Association; the *Outstanding Women in Medicine Award* of the Women's Day Committee of Second Temple Baptist Church; the *Citation for Outstanding Woman in Medicine* from the Community Advisory Committee of the State University of New York at Buffalo; the *Women Helping Women Award* of the Buffalo Chapter of the National Organization of Women; the 1993 *Citizen of the Year Award* from *The Buffalo News*; the NAACP *Community Service Award*; the *Distinguished Alumni Award* of Bennett Park School No. 32; *Business First*, *Forty Under 40* award (1993); the *Toast of Buffalo Award* of the YMCA of Greater Buffalo (1994); the *Community Service Award* in Medicine from Gamma Phi Omega Chapter, Alpha Kappa Alpha Sorority, Inc.; and, with her husband, the *Community Service Award* of the Xi Epsilon Omega Chapter of Alpha Kappa Alpha Sorority, Inc.

Dr. Clapp's husband, Michael C. Ezie, is Director of Medicaid Managed Care at Blue Cross and Blue Shield of Western New York. The couple has three daughters, Chinyere, Kelecchi, and Chisara, and one son, Chiemeka.

Catherine Fisher Collins

Dr. Catherine Fisher Collins has a Doctoral degree from the State University of New York at Buffalo where she also received a Master's degree in Allied Health Education, Evaluation, and Curriculum Development. She is a Pediatric Nurse Practitioner and the first African American nurse practitioner to graduate from the University at Buffalo's School of Nursing, Nurse Practitioner program. In addition she holds three certifications in health education. Dr. Collins completed her undergraduate studies at Buffalo State College, were she received a Bachelor of Science degree in Vocational Technical Education, and Trocaire College's Registered Nurse Program.

During her health career, she has held professional positions in planning, education, and administration. She served as Assistant Academic Dean, Department Chair, and Full Professor at Empire State College. She is an Associate Professor who instructs undergraduate and graduate students in health and criminal justice.

She was the producer and host of WIVB's *Health Service Information* program that aired for three years.

Dr. Collins has won many honors and awards from the following organizations: SUNY Best Faculty Fellow, Community Service and Health awards from the Governors of New York and New Jersey, Buffalo Urban League, Alpha Kappa Alpha Sorority, Inc., Jaycees Attica Prison Branch, NAACP, Coalition of 100 Black Women, National Organization of Women, and Jack and Jill of America, Inc., Eastern Region.

She served on the New York State Commission of Corrections Medical Review Board, the first nurse appointed by the governor to this position, which she held for over five years. In this capacity, Dr. Collins was charged with the review of all New York State prisoners' health complaints and deaths.

Her publishing credit includes *The Imprisonment of African American Women* that was honored with the 1997 *Outstanding Academic and Scholarly Award*, African American Women Health and Social Issues. While serving as National Editor for Jack and Jill of

America Inc., she produced two publications, *Up The Hill 1999 and 2000*. She is under contract for three new books entitled *Stress in the African American Women* (Greenwood Publishing Group), *South Africa Women Prisoners*, and *Prisoners: African American Women* (McFarland Publishing Group).

She serves as Field Reader of grants for the federal government's Department of Health and Human Services, and Reader for Educational Testing Service, College Board's Advance Placement Program.

In 1999, she traveled to South Africa to lecture at the University of South Africa Law School where Nelson Mandela received his law degree. During her visit she completed research for a book and videotaped two women prisons. She has produced two South Africa videos that document her work and visit. In 2000, she traveled to Nigeria to establish two chapters of Jack and Jill of America, Inc.

Dr. Collins is a member of several community groups including Buffalo Links, Naomi Chapters #10 Order of the Eastern Star PHA, Hadji Court #62, Daughters of Isis, NAACP Executive Board, and Buffalo Chapter of Jack and Jill of America, Inc. She has served as president of the local Chapter of Jack and Jill and brought the Beautillion program that honors outstanding African American for their sponsorship.

She has held several positions for Jack and Jill of America including Eastern Regions' Director (1993-1995), National Editor (1998-2000), and currently National Vice President (2000-2002).

Dr. Collins is the mother of Clyde Collins, a State University at New York student; Mrs. Laura Harris, a Buffalo public school administrator; and Tim Austin, an 8th grader. She is the wife of the late Clyde Collins; sister of the late Herman Fisher, Jr.; daughter of the late Herman Fisher and Catherine Lynch Fisher; and sister of Fay Austin and David Fisher. She attends Lincoln Memorial United Methodist Church.

Elaine Hennie-Megna, DDS

Dr. Hennie-Megna is a native of the Bronx, New York. She earned a Bachelor of Science degree at Hunter College. In 1974, she moved to Buffalo to attend Dental School at the University at Buffalo School of Dental Medicine. She established her private practice in 1989 and continues to offer services in cosmetic and general dentistry. She states that her objective is, "to deliver quality care, cost effectively to the Buffalo community."

Since 1985, she also has served as an instructor in the Dental Assisting Program at UB's Educational Opportunity Center.

She is the Past President of the National Dental Association and member of the Upstate Medical Alliance, Eighth District Dental Society, and American Dental Association. She also is a member of Delta Sigma Theta Sorority, Inc.

Dr. Hennie-Megna writes a column on dental health for *The Buffalo Challenger* newspaper. In addition she is a frequent lecturer and guest speaker to high school and college groups. She is a lecturer for the Junior Achievement Program, and is a golf instructor for inner city youth.

Dr. Hennie-Megna is married to Ralph C. Megna, Esq., and has two children, Camille and Brandon.

Thelma C. Hurd

 Dr. Thelma C. Hurd earned her medical degree (1983) and completed residency training (1990) in General Surgery at the University of Medicine and Dentistry of New Jersey, Newark. She completed a clinical fellowship in Surgical Oncology at Ohio State University, Columbus, Ohio. Dr. Hurd moved to Buffalo in 1997 to join the staff of Roswell Park Cancer Institute as Attending Surgeon, Division of Breast Surgery, Department of Surgery. She is licensed by the states of New York, New Jersey, and Texas, and was certified by the American Board of Surgery in 1991 and re-certified in 2001.

Her research interest focuses on breast cancer in African Americans and phenotypic alterations in MHC Class 1 expressions. She has authored or co-authored more than twenty journal publications, book chapters, and abstracts. She is an ad hoc reviewer for *Cancer Research*, *Cancer*, *Archives of Surgery*, and *Journal of Surgical Oncology*.

Dr. Hurd is a member of many professional organizations, including the American Medical Association, American College of Surgeons, Society of Surgical Oncology, Association of Women in Science, and American Society of Breast Disease. She serves on committees at Roswell Park Cancer Institute and the University at Buffalo where she also is an Assistant Professor of Surgery in the School of Medicine and Biomedical Sciences.

She is the recipient of numerous awards including Alpha Kappa Alpha Sorority, Inc., Xi Epsilon Omega Chapter *Health Award*; Who's Who; Kevin Guest House *Heart Award*; Best Doctors in America, *Best Doctors in America – Central Region*, NCI *Minority Scientists Travel Award*; American Cancer Society Oncology Fellowship and Phi Theta Kappa.

In the short time that she has been in Buffalo, Dr. Hurd has been very involved in the community, particularly contributing her expertise on the subject of cancers affecting women. She is a sought after workshop presenter and keynote speaker. She is gratified by the impact that she has had on raising awareness about the issue of cancer to the community and helping those affected through The Witness Project of Buffalo. This community-based breast and cervical cancer education program was implemented to educate African American Women in Buffalo about the importance of breast and cervical cancer screening and diagnosis, and to increase utilization of existing breast and cervical cancer screening programs. Dr. Hurd also is actively engaged in cancer research and is the recipient of numerous grants to advance this segment of her work.

Dr. Juanita K. Hunter

Juanita K. Hunter is a graduate of Buffalo's Hutchinson Central High School. She wanted to attend college. "I grew up in a family of five girls," she said, "and it wasn't a time when we were encouraged to go to school. It did require a bit of determination."

She chose nursing because she could earn a degree more quickly. "I knew four years was beyond my means, and nursing was a suitable alternative," said Dr. Hunter. "Once I got into it, I found it to be quite a challenge."

After graduation from the former Edward J. Meyer Memorial School of Nursing, she worked as a staff nurse there and within two years was appointed head nurse of a medical unit and recognized early as a role model for other nurses and for her activities as a patient advocate.

In 1978, she joined the University of Buffalo faculty, coming from the Veteran's Administration Hospital where she was a public health nurse coordinator. She has advanced degrees in community health nursing and curriculum planning from UB.

Dr. Hunter was married to the late Archie Louis Hunter, a social worker who was active in the community. They had three children, all of whom have completed master's degrees: Jeffrey Alan, a Certified Public Accountant with the National Endowment for Democracy; Wayne Bernard, a staff analyst for Rochester Telephone; and Gail Deneen; who is a graduate from the law school at the University of North Carolina at Chapel Hill.

Though Dr. Hunter got into nursing by chance, she has affirmed the choice repeatedly and has been honored extensively by her peers for contributions to the field. Dr. Hunter has been active in numerous local, state, and national professional organizations. She served, most recently, as the president of the New York State Nurses' Association.

When asked if she would recommend nursing to those making a choice today?

"I think nursing has a lot of promise," she said. "More than ever we need qualified people who are highly creative people because I don't think we can envision what health care will be like in twenty-five years."

Catherine J. Lewis

Catherine J. Lewis is founder of LEWAC (Lasting Education for Women, Adults, and Children) Associates of Western New York, Inc., a health education and wellness agency located at 1490 Jefferson Avenue. She has been CEO and Executive Director since the organization's March 1991 inception. LEWAC provides "ways to wellness" health education, outreach, and awareness workshops and seminars throughout the city of Buffalo, targeting residents of the Masten, Ellicott, and Niagara Districts and utilizes a staff of six people and a speaker's bureau of several physicians and other health care professionals and volunteers.

She has organized health education programs on health and wellness at various community-based sites including Walls Memorial AME Church, Antioch Baptist Church, Mt. Olive Baptist Church, The New Mt. Ararat Church, Bethel AME Church, First Shiloh Baptist Church, Calvary Baptist Church, LBJ Housing Development, First Shiloh Housing Corporation, and many others who call upon the LEWAC Team to complement a wellness in mind, body, and spirit.

Ms. Lewis served in management and administrative capacities in the health care industry since 1964, including Buffalo General Hospital, Blue Cross and Blue Shield of Western New York, and Blue Cross and Blue Shield of New York City.

She served as Delegation Services Manager for the World University Games held in Buffalo (July 1993). In this capacity she was responsible for coordinating and registering eight thousand athletes from 130 different countries, and coordinating the training of over one thousand volunteers. She serves as a volunteer in numerous community projects including the United Way of Buffalo and Erie County Speaker's Bureau.

She was chosen as a recipient of the American Diabetes Association's *Women of Valor* award, a community-based initiative recognizing woman of outstanding achievement in their local community. *Business First* recognized Ms. Lewis as one of Buffalo and Western New York's Health Heroes for the year 2000.

She is an advocate for health and wellness and serves on a number of panels and forums where health issues, including environmental health issues, impact communities of color. She is an active participant of the American Diabetes Association Cultural Diversity Initiatives. In addition, she is a Buffalo Prep Board of Trustee member; the Erie County Legislature Task Force Chairperson; and was elected President of the Erie County Chapter of The Links, Incorporated. She is a member of Antioch Baptist Church.

Ms. Lewis holds a Bachelor of Science degree in Business Administration from New York University with course studies at the University of Buffalo, Syracuse University, and Bryant and Stratton Business Institute.

Pashion Corbitt Marshall

Pashion Payton Corbitt is a native of Buffalo, and a graduate of the former East High School. She received her Bachelor of Science degree in Pharmacy at Northeastern University in Boston, Massachusetts; and completed some courses in the Master of Business Administration Program from the State University of New York at Buffalo. She holds licensure in the states of New York and Massachusetts, and has been a pharmacist in local facilities for the past three decades. She has maintained her current pharmacy position at the Daughters of Charity Hospital (Sisters Hospital) for several years, providing in-service education to medical and technical staff, monitoring patient medication profiles, filling prescriptions, and is a liaison to the neonatal department at the hospital. She formerly served as a pharmacist at NCS Healthcare (Eckerd Drugs) where she processed and filled medication and medical supply orders for nursing homes, correctional facilities, group homes, and convent accounts.

She is a scientist, mentor, administrator, and community leader. As Director of Pharmacy for Sheehan Memorial Hospital, she developed a Policy and Procedure manual, created a formulary and revised the exchange cart system used in the Unit Dose Distribution System, revised the IV administration system, and the total parenteral nutrition program. As the Director of Pharmacy at the Western New York Children's Psychiatric Center, she implemented the Unit Dose Drug Distribution system, prepared the Pharmacy for accreditation by the Joint Commission on Accreditation of Hospital Organizations (JCAHO) and other accrediting bodies, and maintained a Quality Assurance Program for Pharmacy Services. At Geneva General Hospital, she developed a Unit Dose Drug Distribution System, set up the IV Admixture System for antibiotic piggybacks, created and edited the *Pharmacy Newsletter*, and established criteria for use of Total Parenteral Nutrition.

In 2002, Ms. Marshall received The *Silver Beaver Award* from the National Court of Honor, Boy Scouts of America in recognition of her exceptional and noteworthy service to that organization. She also is the recipient of the *Whitney M. Young, Jr. Award* (Boy Scouts of America); the *1490 Jefferson Enterprises Black Achievers in Industry Award*; and the Southern Christian Leadership Conference (SCLC) *Martin Luther King, Jr. Community Service Award*. She has received the Boy Scouts of America's Greater Niagara Frontier Council District *Award of Merit*; the Boy Scouts of America *Woodbadge Award*; and the *Woman of the Year* award from the American Business Women Association.

She has spent her life being instrumental in organizing and planning fundamental programs to advance young people in the pharmacy profession. At The State University of New York at Buffalo, she has provided lectures to pre-pharmacy students regarding her experiences and year after year she was rated as the top speaker. She created a training program site (S.T.E.P.) for high school students at Sheehan Memorial Hospital and is a former member of SUNY at Buffalo's Minority Student Advisory Board. As Director of Sheehan, she has provided guidance and internship opportunities for both pre-pharmacy and pharmacy students. She is responsible for starting and setting up the SUNY AB Educational Opportunity Center's first Pharmacy Technician Training Program, which included women in 1995. This consisted of program structure, guidelines for certification, lesson plans, hiring and supervision of staff, and final determination of program requirements for participants' graduation.

She is past president of the American Business Women's Association, Frontier Chapter; Committee Chairperson, Boy Scouts of America for Troop and Pack 84 since 1983; Advisory Board member and former Executive Board member, Greater Niagara Frontier Council, Boy Scouts of America (1988-91); Alumni Recruiter, Minority Student Advisory Board member (SUNY at Buffalo), Northeastern University since 1988; a member of the Western New York Society of Health Systems Pharmacists since 1985; and one of the founding members of Project WIN (Women Issues Network). She is a member of the United Voices of St. John Baptist Church Choir, Building Committee Member and former co-chairwoman of Youth Fellowship and Task Force member for St. John Christian Academy. She also is a member of Alpha Kappa Alpha Sorority Inc., Gamma Phi Omega Chapter.

She is constantly encouraging those who come in contact with her to pursue their dreams in the sciences. She has provided enthusiastic support to hundreds of peers, professionals, and students. She is a woman of strong character, yet she has a gentle spirit that resonates compassion and sensitivity. People are attracted to her by her undeniable warmth and effervescent personality. She seeks no recognition or accolades for what she does. She is a human heart, which is evidenced, through her work and her dedication to her profession. She has made her mark in the field of Pharmacy by her goal-oriented attitude and her faith, despite the fact it is a male-dominated profession. She was the first member of her nuclear family to attend and graduate from college and she continues to put one foot in front of the other to reach her desired goals. This is the philosophy she projects to others as well. She has been a role model not only to her son, Kyle Francis Corbitt, throughout his life and college endeavors; she is a role model for everyone who is blessed to know her. In her leisure time she enjoys sewing, scouting, and traveling. It also is ironic that one of her hobbies is gardening; as when God planted her as a seed in His Garden of Life, He already knew she was designated to become an American Beauty Rose.

Pashion also shares her life and accomplishments with her husband, Anthony L. Marshall.

Eva M. Noles

Mrs. Eva M. Noles is a Registered Nurse, a Nursing Educator, and a former Director of Nursing at Buffalo's world-renowned Roswell Park Cancer Institute. The first black nurse to train in Buffalo, Mrs. Noles has retired twice only to return to train people to provide various levels of health care. She was with the Roswell Park Cancer Institute for some thirty years, serving in many capacities; with the Medical Personnel Pool for seven years, training nurses aides, and helping educate more than one hundred others as family planning nurse practitioners.

She recalls that nursing was not always a career choice opened to blacks. In 1936, when she applied to the Buffalo City Hospital's three-year diploma nursing school, blacks were not accepted. On a dare from a friend, Mrs. Noles applied and to her surprise, was accepted. It was a case, she believes, of being in the right place at the right time. But if it was a stroke of luck, which resulted in her timely application, it was hard work and a fight against racial discrimination that enabled her to succeed.

Although she was admitted to the nursing program at the hospital that later became E.J. Meyer, and today the Erie County Medical Center, she was not fully accepted in the school and encountered many subtle forms of racial prejudice. At the senior dinner dance, Mrs. Noles and her date were asked to leave. The only blacks allowed at such events, it seemed, were the serving people. Mrs. Noles and her companion did not fit this category.

Prejudice did not end with her diploma from the School of Nursing. It followed her into her first years of working at her profession. As the first black staff nurse to be hired at RPMI, however, her courage and determination led her up the ladder to become a head nurse. Pushing a bit harder, she was named an instructor of nursing and then assistant director of nursing. During her last three years at RPMI, she became Director of Nursing. Today, in addition to having earned the R.N. designation, she also holds a Bachelor of Science degree in nursing from the State University at Buffalo and the Master of Arts degree in education.

After retiring from RPMI, Mrs. Noles worked on a federal grant to train nurse practitioners. Later joining Medical Personnel Pool as a home care supervisor, she then was named staff developer for the firm. Today, she is busy training nurses' aides through a state training grant. Mrs. Noles' early education at Hutchinson Central High School, now Hutchinson Technical High School, included courses in mathematics, science, and chemistry, which were prerequisites for nursing education.

Today, Mrs. Noles serves on the New York State Board of Nursing the New York State Nurses Association District One, and has been an active member of the American Nurses Association (ANA) and many of its national committees. The responsibilities she has had in connection with the ANA have given her the opportunity to attend meetings around the world, which in turn have allowed her to share her knowledge of nursling's growing role in health care. Mrs. Noles has served on the Buffalo General Hospital Board of Trustees, she has been the chairwoman of the governing board of the Community

Mental Health Center of the hospital, and she has been a member of the Board of Directors for the Greater Buffalo Chapter of the American Red Cross.

Her service as a volunteer with the local American Red Cross has earned her a national award, and her contributions to nursing and her community have garnered her many others. The Medical Personnel Pool has established a five-year scholarship and the New York State Nurses Association, District One, will present it in Mrs. Noles' name at its annual dinner each year. The scholarship will be awarded to an outstanding senior minority nursing student in Western New York.

She estimates her volunteer work accounted for at least one-third of her time prior to retirement and now takes at least three-quarters. In addition, she still makes time for her home and family.

Despite her current responsibilities, she spends as much time as possible continuing to help others. Struggling against impressive odds and coming out on top has been a pattern for Mrs. Noles, but she insists it has been more than a matter of luck.

"Success is hard work," she says, "and getting an education is number one. Then using this knowledge to gain what you want and being prepared is the key." She adds, however, that being broadminded and overlooking some of the remarks and innuendoes also will help people reach their goals.

Mrs. Noles is sister to another Uncrowned Queen, Donnie Dukes.

Vernette Coles Patterson

Vernette Coles Patterson was born August 2, 1925, in Bellevue, Pennsylvania. She attended Elementary and High Schools in Pittsburgh, Pennsylvania. She also attended Mercy Hospital and School for Nurses in Philadelphia from 1943 to 1945. She later attended Millard Fillmore College in Buffalo.

Ms. Patterson worked for almost thirty years as a Cardiopulmonary Technologist in the Angiology Department of Buffalo General Hospital, Diagnostic Cardiovascular Laboratory. From 1972 to 1987, she was a Research Technician at the State University of New York at Buffalo, Buffalo General Hospital.

She is a member of the National Society of Cardiopulmonary Technologists, Inc. Her civic and service organization affiliations include: East Side Community Organization, Inc., ESCO (Board of Directors); Planned Parenthood of Buffalo, Inc. (Board of Directors); Westminster Community House, Inc. (Board of Directors); Buffalo Chapter of The Links, Incorporated (forty-two years); African Cultural Center; Buffalo Negro Scholarship Foundation; Buffalo Federation of Women's Clubs; Women in Community Service (WICS); Research Institute on Alcoholism (Committee on Human Subjects); Black Dance Workshop, Inc. (Board of Directors); Buffalo General Hospital Institutional Review (Board Member); NCCJ National Conference for Community Justice (Board Member); Volunteer Women for Human Rights and Dignity (WHRD); Afro-American Historical Association of the Niagara Frontier, Inc. (Member); NAACP (Life Member); Deaconess Center (Volunteer); National Society of Cardiopulmonary Technologists, Inc. (Member).

Mrs. Patterson is a member of Lincoln Memorial United Methodist Church where she has been active for over thirty years. Throughout her membership she as served in many of the church's organizations and currently participates as a member of several choirs.

She was married in 1946 to the late James Patterson. They have two children, Gregory James and Kevin LeRoy.

Dr. Lydia T. Wright

Lydia T. Wright was born on May 5, 1922, in Shreveport, Louisiana. While still a child, Lydia and her sister, twin brothers, and mother, Parthenia Hickman Wright, moved to Cincinnati, Ohio, to join her father, Nathan, who was forced to flee Louisiana to escape lynching.

She attended the University of Cincinnati and Fisk University in Nashville. She received her medical degree from Meharry Medical College, also in Nashville. Dr. Wright completed her residency in New York City where she met her husband, Dr. Frank G. Evans. They were married in 1951, and relocated to Buffalo the following year.

Dr. Wright has several notable firsts on her resume. She was the first African American pediatrician and female physician in Buffalo. She also was the first black person appointed to serve on the Buffalo Board of Education, an office she assumed in May 1962. She served a five-year term on the Board, but declined a reappointment in 1967, noting that the education system was moving forward.

In an interview with *The Buffalo Challenger* newspaper, Dr. Wright recalled her tenure on the school board. She is remembered for her stand, as the lone opponent to the then Board majority's decision to establish a virtually all-black enrollment for Woodlawn Junior High School. "They drew the attendance lines to segregate the schools," she said. Dr. Wright is described in the article as being the "community's voice during board debates on school racial integration." In September 2000, the Common Council passed a resolution, sponsored by Council member Charley H. Fisher, to name the future school building proposed at the Kensington Heights site for Dr. Wright. A public hearing to celebrate the naming of the school after Dr. Wright was held on September 25, 2000, at Buffalo City Hall.

Dr. Wright also served on the board of the East Side Community Organization, Inc. (ESCO), the group that brought Saul Alinsky to Buffalo to organize Buffalo's black community. Dr. Wright and ESCO played an important role in bridging the gap between the black and white communities. She also was a member of the Committee for an Urban University in the Downtown Area.

Dr. Wright and her husband are members of St. Philip's Episcopal Church where she served on the Altar Guild. She has served on the Race Relations Committee of the Council of Churches and also was the first woman in the United States to be appointed to an Episcopal Bishop's standing committee, by the late Rt. Reverend Lauriston Scaife. Her other firsts include being the first black to receive the coveted *Red Jacket Award* from the Buffalo and Erie County Historical Society, the first recipient of the *Barber G. Conable Award* from the Citizen's Council on Human Relations, and the *Pediatrician of the Year Award* from the Buffalo Pediatric Society. She also is a recipient of the *Brotherhood Award* of the National Conference of Christians and Jews.

Dr. Wright is a family historian, having traced her family history to the 11th century, and has developed a huge family history chart that proudly displays her lineage. She comes from a long line of educators dating back to her grandparents. Her maternal grandmother was a teacher, as was her mother, who graduated from the University of Cincinnati. Her father was a graduate of Tuskegee Institute and her maternal grandfather, Dr. Benjamin Hickman, was one of the first blacks to practice medicine in Cincinnati.

Dr. Wright and her husband have two children: Tamara, an attorney in Los Angeles, and Frank Jr., a local stockbroker, and two grandsons.

Uncrowned Queen Historians

Lillion Batchelor

Lillion Batchelor founded Buffalo Quarters Historical Society in 1995. Her purpose was to increase National and International awareness of the significant role of Buffalo in the Underground Railroad movement. The Society presents annual recreations of historical events through drama and music culminating in the Niagara River Crossing into Fort Erie, Ontario, Canada.

Ms. Batchelor has worked to bring about a sense of hope, pride, and recognition to Western New York by presenting historical truths, honoring unsung heroes, expanding historical research, increasing international awareness of Buffalo's role in the Underground Railroad, and sharing this rich history in drama, music, and literature.

Through her research, she has discovered and is now cultivating a precious gem in her Broderick Park Project. Construction is now underway to transform Broderick Park into an International Freedom Memorial Park that will compliment ongoing educational efforts.

She founded the only organization (the Buffalo Quarters Historical Society) that utilizes the Niagara River to promote the history of the Underground Railroad in the Buffalo area in partnership with the Canadian government. Under her leadership, the organization has received accolades from United States and Canadian leaders.

Among her numerous awards, Ms Batchelor has received the *Civic Empowerment Award* (2000); Outstanding Planning Project – Underground Railroad Freedom Memorial (1999); The Municipal Council of the Town of Fort Erie *Award of Appreciation* (1998); the *William Wells Brown Award* (1996); Proclamations from the State of New York (1997), City of Buffalo (1995), and City of Fort Erie, Canada (1995).

Among her greatest contributions to the world is her example of parenting. As a grandparent, she has shaped and sculptured replicas of herself through her granddaughters, molding her legacy to ensure that the torch is carried for future generations.

Florence Hargrave Curtis

Florence Hargrave Curtis, a native of Buffalo, is the daughter of the late Ashley S. and Annie Whitehead Hargrave. She began her education in the Buffalo Public Schools. She has an Associate's degree in Applied Sciences and Nursing from Erie Community College; a Bachelor of Science degree in Community and Human Services with a concentration in Studies in Chemical Dependence; and a Master of Arts degree in Culture and Policy Studies. She is the mother of one daughter, Dawn C. Roberts, and the grandmother of three, Alvin, Alicia, and John Roberts.

Florence's fascination with her second great-grandmother, Landonia Epps, led to her most unprecedented scholarly achievement, *Daughter Be Somebody* - a book that traces her family's history from 1740 through 1997. It is a testament to the strength of the human spirit and the determination of two families to break the shackles of slavery and overcome its legacy through knowledge and education. It is a powerful and dramatic source of genealogical information that warms the heart, brings tears to ones eyes, but most of all it takes the reader on a magnificent journey into yesterday.

For Ms. Curtis, there is nothing about which she is more passionate than African American history. For this reason, she has written five other books. Three of these books are tools for the researcher to make their search a little easier and help knock down the brick wall that every historian confronts in his or her search. The other two, *He Heard My Cry* and *Everlasting Memories* are books of original inspirational poetry.

Ms. Curtis has searched her maternal lineage back to 1066 AD and her paternal ancestry back to 1634 AD. For her, the search never ends for there are always new roads to explore and new visions of old materials to document. In addition to *Daughter Be Somebody*, she has written *He Heard My Cry*; *Landonia Epps, a Paper Trail of Her Times and Travels*; *Halifax Country, North Carolina Coroner's Inquests 1841-1891*; *Everlasting Memories*; and *In the Footsteps of Our Forefathers, the Churches Where They Worshipped, the Graves In Which They Slumber*. Her books have found a home at the Schomburg Center for research in Black Culture; Duke University's John Hope Franklin Research Center for African and African American Documentation; Virginia State University; Saint Paul's College, Lawrenceville, Virginia; Halifax County, North Carolina Library; as well as other educational venues.

Ms. Curtis has spoken at numerous universities and for many genealogical societies on the importance and value of family research.

She notes, "I have searched the pages of the past for a glimpse into yesterday, to make sense of today, and to find meaning in tomorrow."

Lillian S. Williams

Lillian S. Williams was born in Vicksburg, Mississippi, and was raised in Niagara Falls, New York, where her family moved when she was four years old. She is the oldest of nine children of Ada L. Williams and the late James L. Williams, Sr.

Committed to public education, Williams proudly acknowledges that she attended the public schools of Niagara Falls where she graduated with a New York State Regents diploma with four years' honors in mathematics, science, English, Social Studies, and Latin. She earned her Bachelor of Arts, Master of Arts, and Doctor of Philosophy degrees from the University at Buffalo, The State University of New York, where she majored in history.

She is a dedicated teacher, scholar, and community activist. Currently, she is Chair of the Department of African American Studies at the University at Buffalo, The State University of New York. Prior to this position, she was an associate professor at the University at Albany, SUNY, where she taught in the Women's Studies Department and directed the Institute for Research on Women. Her passion is history and she especially is committed to preserving the records of African Americans. While still a graduate student, she was a founder of the African American Historical Society of the Niagara Frontier and associate editor of its journal, *Afro-Americans in New York Life and History*. She is editor of the papers for the National Association of Colored Women's Clubs, the oldest secular African American organization still in existence.

Dr. Williams is the author of the highly acclaimed *Strangers in the Land of Paradise: The Creation of an African American Community, Buffalo, New York, 1900-1925* published by Indiana University Press in 1999 and released in paperback in 2000. The monograph *A Bridge to the Future: the History of Diversity in Girl Scouting* which she prepared for Girl Scouts of America led to her current book project tentatively titled *Blacks in Green: African Americans and the Girl Scout Movement*. She is the biographer of turn-of-the-twentieth-century-Buffalo reformer Mary Burnett Talbert. Williams' other scholarly projects include historian consultant for the New York State Museum's permanent exhibition *Black Capital: Harlem in the 1920s*, the New York State Archive exhibit *The Union Preserved: New York in the Civil War*; and associate editor of the *Encyclopedia of New York State*.

Her parents stressed the importance of involvement in her community and a commitment to social change. She served as a member of the mayor's technical advisory committee for the District of Columbia's Twenty-Year Comprehensive Plan, and she was an expert witness in a federal lawsuit that the NAACP litigated. She is a member of the board of directors of the Albany NAACP. She served on the Education Committee of the Buffalo Urban League and the New York State Historic Records Advisory Board.

Dr. Williams has received several awards for her professional and service contributions. She is the recipient of the *SUNY Chancellor's Award for Excellence in Teaching*; the Niagara County Black Achievers' awarded her the *Lifetime Achievement* award (2000); and she was selected as a fellow in the 2001 National African American Women's Leadership Institute.

Uncrowned Queens in
Legal Services and Law Enforcement

Marian Bass

Marian Bass, a retired Captain of the Buffalo Police Department, was a trailblazer for women in law enforcement. She was Buffalo's first permanent, minority woman officer and the first woman Lieutenant and Captain of Police. She is the only woman in Western New York certified as a candidate for Inspector of Police (the highest civil service rank in law enforcement), and the only woman in Western New York to have commanded a police precinct.

She earned four degrees subsequent to her appointment that include a Master of Arts degree in Criminal Justice from the Rockefeller College of Public Affairs and Policy, and a Master of Science degree in Urban Affairs from the State University of New York at Buffalo. She has served as a Guardian Ad Litem in Family Court, Senior Arbitrator for the Better Business Bureau, Matrimonial Fee Arbitration panel member in Supreme Court, and as a substitute teacher for BOCES. She also was an interviewer for Channel 18's *Fifteen Minutes of Fortune and Fame* program.

A prolific writer on police subjects, she has been published both locally and nationally. As Commander of the Crime Prevention Bureau, she and her staff were featured in *EBONY* magazine for excellence in law enforcement. She is a motivational speaker for young people and frequent graduation speaker. In 2000, she became a Canisius College certified Paralegal.

Captain Bass is a 1490 Black Achiever and recipient of the *YMCA Leadership Award*. In 1993, the Better Business Bureau of Western New York nominated her *Arbitrator of the Year*. The University Community Council of State University of New York at Buffalo cited her as *Outstanding Woman in the Professions in Western New York*. In 1984, she received the University's *Distinguished Alumnus* award. A former adjunct professor at Erie Community College, she received a *Distinguished Alumnus* award from that institution in 1998. In the same year, she also received an award from the Erie County Sheriff's Foundation for excellence in law enforcement. She also received the

Sojourner Truth Award from the National Association of Negro Business and Professional Women, Buffalo Club.

She has a special rapport with disadvantaged youth and at-risk students. She is the daughter of Ray Bass (deceased) who was formerly the largest minority contractor in Western New York. In the 1930s her father was the first Afro-American admitted into the Building Trades Union.

She is known for cultivating beautiful gardens around her home in Amherst. Her memberships include, Working for Downtown, American Association of University Women, UB Women's Club, Afro-American Historical Association of the Niagara Frontier, Police Conference of Western New York, New York State Dispute Resolution Association, and the Western New York Association of Retired Police Officers. She is fourth Vice President of the Judges and Police Conference of Western New York. Captain Bass is a member of Bethel AME Church.

Tearah Grace Mullins, Esq.

Ms. Mullins is a 1983 graduate of the State University of New York at Buffalo. She earned a Bachelor of Arts degree in Spanish and is a 1986 graduate of UB's School of Law. A Buffalo resident, Ms. Mullins began her legal career at the law firm of Siegel, Kelleher and Kahn, where she worked exclusively on matrimonial and family law matters.

In 1988, Ms. Mullins was appointed to the position of Court Attorney to the Buffalo City Court Judges. She was the first African American to receive this position. In 1999, Attorney Mullins was appointed by the Honorable Thomas P. Amodeo, Chief Judge of Buffalo City Court, to the position of Supervising Court Attorney of the Buffalo City Court Legal Staff. Attorney Mullins also has served as Confidential Law Clerk to the Honorable Rose H. Sconiers. Supreme Court Justice, 8th Judicial District, and was the first African American woman in Erie County to serve as Law Clerk in State Supreme Court.

119

Having served as Court Attorney to the City Court Judges for well over a decade, Ms. Mullins has handled countless issues, both civil and criminal, that have come before the court. This experience has provided her with an in-depth knowledge of City Court, including its specialized courts (housing, domestic violence, drug). Attorney Mullins also has experience on the bench, having served as Hearing Officer in the Domestic Violence Court under the Honorable E. Jeannette Ogden.

She is a former member of the Board of Directors of the Buffalo Urban League. In addition, she is a current member of the Board of Directors of the Erie County Bar Association's Aid to Indigent Prisoners Program and the program's Appellate Subcommittee.

She is active in the Minority Bar Association, serving as President, Vice-President, and Treasurer of the organization. The theme of her Presidency has been for the members to "leave their ivory towers, roll up their sleeves, and become directly involved in the affairs of the community." To that end, Ms. Mullins established The President's Fund to provide gifts and financial assistance to needy families and charities. To date, the Minority Bar Association adopted two families through the Buffalo Municipal Housing Authority's Adopt-A-Family program; donated money to Project Joy, Phase II that provides Christmas Toys to local children; and donated money toward a Christmas Toy giveaway at Children's Hospital. The organization also donated money to Durham Memorial AME Zion Church to help them feed the poor; donated money toward an effort to provide clothing, toys, and food to a refugee family from Sierra Leone; and also donated money to The Cornerstone Manner, to help purchase toys and games for the children of displaced mothers. Ms. Mullins also served on the "First Annual Millennium Awards Committee" for *The Buffalo Challenger* in order to raise money to benefit the Community newspaper.

Judge E. Jeannette Ogden

E. Jeannette Ogden is a Buffalo City Court Judge presently presiding over the Domestic Violence Court. Mayor Anthony M. Masiello appointed Judge Ogden to the Court in June of 1995. He cited her broad based experience in the law as the basis for her appointment. In November of 1995, she was elected to serve a ten-year term on the City Court. She has handled thousands of civil and criminal cases since her appointment to the bench and has developed the reputation of being a no nonsense Judge.

Prior to her appointment, Judge Ogden worked as a trial attorney for CIGNA Insurance Company where she defended corporations, school districts, hospitals, and municipalities while at the same time operating her own private law practice. She also is a former Prosecutor from the Erie County District Attorney's Office and a former Assistant County Attorney.

Judge Ogden is a graduate of Buffalo Public Schools and Buffalo State College, where she earned a Bachelor of Science degree in Criminal Justice and presently teaches. She received her Juris Doctorate Degree from the University at Buffalo, School of Law and also instructs courses in Trial Technique and Mental Health Issues in Criminal Law.

Her professional affiliations include memberships on the Advisory Committee on Judicial Ethics, the Gender and Racial Fairness Committee for the Courts, and the New York State and American Association of Women Judges. She is a member and past President of the Women Lawyers of Western New York, Co-Chairperson of the Diversity Committee of the Women's Bar Association of Western New York and a member of various other Bar Associations.

Hard work and community service have always been important values to the Judge. She is a former member of the Erie Community College Board of Trustees; the Board of Directors of the Girl Scouts of America, Inc.; Legal Services for the Elderly and Disabled; Indigent Prisoners Association; and Sheehan Memorial Hospital. She also provided free legal services to many local churches, community based organizations, and block clubs.

Judge Ogden presently serves as a mentor to students in elementary, high school, college, and law school. She is a member of the Erie County Chapter of The Links, Incorporated; the Women's Group; Business and Professional Women's Association; NAACP, Mt. Olive Development Corp.; and the League of Women Voters.

Judge Ogden is the recipient of many awards and acknowledgement for her long-standing community involvement. She exemplifies the product of hard work, perseverance, and commitment. She attributes all of her accomplishments to the support of a loving family and a strong belief in God. She is a member of the Mt. Olive Baptist Church and resides in Buffalo with her family.

Honorable Rose H. Sconiers

Honorable Rose H. Sconiers, New York State Supreme Court Justice, is former judge of the City Court of Buffalo; former Executive Attorney of the Legal Aid Bureau of Buffalo, Inc.; former Assistant Corporation Counsel for the City of Buffalo; and a 1973 graduate of the State University of New York at Buffalo School of Law. She was admitted to the State Board in 1974, and to the United States Federal District Court in 1975. In addition, she is admitted to the United States Court of Appeals for the Second Circuit and the United States Supreme Court.

Justice Sconiers is an emeritus member of the University at Buffalo Council and a past President of the New York State Association of Council Members and College Trustees. She was appointed by the Chief Judge of New York State to the Unified Court System Advisory Committee on Criminal Law and Procedure and the Jury Project. She also is a member of the Franklin H. Williams Judicial Commission on Minorities. Justice Sconiers is past president of the University at Buffalo Law Alumni Association and a former member of the Board of Directors of the New York State Defenders Association.

Justice Sconiers is the first Vice President of the Association of Justices of the Supreme Court of the State of New York; Assistant Presiding Officer of the Judicial Council of the New York State Bar Association; and a delegate to the National Conference of State Trial Judges of the American Bar Association.

She is a member of the Board of Directors of the Erie County Bar Foundation; a former member of the Erie County Bar Association Grievance Committee; and the past Chairman of the Lawyer Referral Service Committee and Law Day Committee. She also served on the Bar's Special Committee to Study the Feasibility of Creating a Police Civilian Review Board for the Buffalo Police Department; Practice and Procedure in City Court Committee; Judiciary Committee; and Ethics Committee.

Justice Sconiers is a Past President of the Erie County Chapter of The Links, Incorporated; past President of the Supreme Court Justices Association, Eighth Judicial District; past President of the Buffalo Chapter, National Bar Association; past Chairperson, Friends of The School of Architecture and Environmental Design at SUNY; past Vice-Chairperson, Women for Downtown; past President, Community Planning and Assistance Center for Western New York (CPAC); and past Chairperson of the 13th Street Multi-Purpose Center, Inc., in Niagara Falls, New York. Justice Sconiers is a former member of the Board of Trustees of Children's Hospital; the Board of Trustees of St. Mary School for the Deaf; and Board of Directors of the Buffalo Chapter, American Red Cross.

Justice Sconiers is married to Attorney Lester G. Sconiers and is the mother of a daughter, Lisa Rose, and son, Lester, Jr.

Barbara M. Sims

Barbara M. Sims has enjoyed a career both as a school teacher and as an attorney. Just before attending the State University of New York at Buffalo, School of Law, she passed the citywide teacher's examination with the highest score and placed first on the list of qualified applicants.

Shortly thereafter she became the first African American women to receive a law degree at UB. Upon graduating from Law school she entered into a law partnership with her husband, the late Judge William Sims, under the firm name of Sims and Sims, were she engaged in private practice for several years.

Judge Sims was recruited to join the Office of the District Attorney of Erie County, becoming the first African American women Assistant District Attorney in Erie County. While acting as an assistant district attorney, she wrote appellate briefs and argued appeals to the Appellate Courts including the Appellate Division and Court of Appeals, the highest court in the State of New York. She also submitted petitions for Certiorari to the United States Supreme Court.

She has been elected to every office in the Women Lawyers Association where she has served as President, Vice-President, Secretary and Treasurer. She also has served as National Vice President to the National Association of Black Women Attorneys headquartered in Washington, D.C.

After leaving the District Attorney's Office, she became a Hearing Officer in the Parking Violations Bureau of the City of Buffalo. While working in that capacity, she was recruited to teach at the University at Buffalo Law School. She also was appointed to the position of Assistant to the President of the University at Buffalo for Minority and Women's Affairs and served as Director of the Office of Equal Opportunity where it was among her responsibilities to further the advancement of women in the disciplines where they had not traditionally been accepted. She also taught courses in the undergraduate division of the University.

After she left UB, she went to work in the Law Offices of Robinson, Sims, Gibson, and Green, which was then located in the Hotel Statler Office Building. It was while in that law office, that she was recruited to run for Associate Judge of the City Court of Buffalo.

During her career, she acted as local Counsel to the NAACP where she represented clients in various civil rights lawsuits, including discrimination in housing and in employment, in addition to criminal matters. Judge Sims has been the recipient of more than fifty awards presented to her for her services to the community and as an attorney.

Currently, she is Counsel to the *Buffalo Criterion* weekly newspaper in which her parents, Frank and Carmelita Merriweather, operated for more than fifty years. In addition to her mother, Barbara's sister, Thyra Merriweather Charles, also is an Uncrowned Queen.

Sharon A. Thomas

On April 1, 1999, Sharon A. Thomas made history when she was elevated to the position of Chief Clerk of Buffalo City Court. Ms. Thomas is the first African American to hold the Chief Clerk position outside the New York City area. She oversees the daily operations of the busiest upstate local criminal courthouse, and is responsible for supervising a staff of eighty-four court employees. As Mayor Anthony M. Masiello told the audience at Ms. Thomas' swearing in ceremony, she attained the position of Chief Clerk "...the old fashion way, she earned it." Ms. Thomas began her court career as an Information Aide under the federally funded CETA program in 1974. She was later named the Deputy Chief Clerk in 1981, a position she held for eighteen years until she was named the Chief Clerk.

Sharon Tomas is a product of the Buffalo Public School system. She earned a Bachelor of Science degree in Business Administration/Education from Daemen College in 1981. She has been certified by the New York State Office of Court Administration as an instructor in Cultural Diversity and Public Awareness courses.

She is well known in the Court system as an innovator and hard worker. She was instrumental in the creation of the Children Center in Buffalo City Court that opened in December 1999 for families that have court-related cases. Sharon is a member of the Office of Court Administration's Gender Bias and Gender Fairness Committee for the 8th Judicial District, and the Co-Chairperson of the Committee for the Development of Domestic Violence Protocols for Supreme, County, Family and City Courts located in Buffalo. She also is on the Commission on Minorities in the Court Advisory Committee.

Sharon is the recipient of the prestigious *Unified Court System Merit Performance Award* (2000), which she received during the Law Day celebration at the State Court of Appeals in Albany.

She has a long history of involvement in many professional and community-based organizations and committees. Currently, she is President of the Board of Directors of the YWCA and also chairs the YWCA's Racial Justice Committee; Secretary of the Board of Directors of Women for Human Rights and Dignity; and serves as a member of the Buffalo and Erie County Public Library Board of Trustees. Sharon is the former Chairperson of the Erie County Commission on the Status of Women. In addition, she is the former President of the Inner City Red Cross Board of Directors, as well as a member of the Regional Board of the Red Cross. Her affiliations and volunteer work are impressive and reveal her genuine desire to help others.

Sharon is the mother of two grown daughters and four grandchildren.

Judge Shirley Troutman

Judge Shirley Troutman is a graduate of Bennett Park School No. 32. She obtained a Bachelor of Science degree in Business Administration from the State University of New York at Buffalo, and a Juris Doctorate degree from Albany Law School of Union University.

Judge Troutman began her legal career in 1986, as an Assistant District Attorney at the Erie County District Attorney's Office, where she served as a prosecutor. In 1989, she joined the New York State Department of Law as Assistant Attorney General where she represented the State of New York in Federal and State Courts as a trial attorney.

In 1992, she joined the United States Department of Justice as an Assistant United States Attorney for the Western District of New York. As an Assistant United States Attorney, Judge Troutman represented the United States in civil litigation matters.

In January 1994, Mayor Anthony M. Masiello appointed Judge Troutman to Buffalo City Court, and in the November election of 1994, she was elected to a full ten-year term. As a Buffalo City Court Judge, she hears thousands of criminal cases per year, including criminal arraignments. She also handles civil cases including many matters transferred from State Supreme Court. Her duties also include a review of small claims cases, landlord tenant, infant settlements, and review of search and arrest warrants.

Judge Troutman is an adjunct professor for the University at Buffalo's Law School. She is a member of the Erie County Bar Association and the Minority Bar Association. Judge Troutman currently serves on the board of St. John Christian Academy and is a past board member of the Women's Bar Association of Western New York.

Judge Troutman speaks on a regular basis at many area schools and lectures for community groups about the court system. She supervises students who participate in the City As School internship program and the Bennett Park School No. 32 Law Magnet Program. She also serves as a Mentor for the Welfare to Work Program sponsored by the New York State Division for Women.

She is a recipient of the *Black Achiever's Award* and the Forty *Under 40* award.

On a personal note, Judge Troutman is the mother of two, Stephen and Lauren.

Garnet Hicks Wallace

Garnet Wallace came to Buffalo to become the Superintendent of the Buffalo Friendship Home in 1947. A graduate of Wilberforce University in Wilberforce, Ohio, she began her career working with youngsters at the Dunbar Nursery School in Syracuse, New York. After leaving Dunbar, she took a position at the Albion Training School for developmentally delayed youngsters. This was during World War II and that position terminated when the former teacher returned from service and reclaimed her position. The loss of this job prompted her move to Buffalo.

Following positions at the Buffalo Psychiatric Center and the Western Reformatory in Albion, New York, Ms. Wallace accepted a position as an institutional parole officer with New York State in 1965. She progressed within the department, being promoted to field parole officer, senior parole officer, and ultimately was selected as the first female to supervise males in the Buffalo area. Eventually, she supervised parole officers in New York City, Manhattan, and North Territory. She retired in 1979 after thirty-two years of service in New York State.

Ms. Wallace has been an active volunteer in the community since her move to Buffalo. Early on she joined the Lit-Mus Study Club and served on numerous committees at the Michigan Avenue YMCA She is an active participant in the work of Bethel AME Church, the Women's Missionary Society, and the First Episcopal District of the AME Church. She is the parliamentarian for the Western New York Conference Branch of the Women's Missionary Society as well as the Historiographer for the Western New York Conference of the African Methodist Episcopal Church.

Other organizations to which she devotes her time and expertise include The Links, Incorporated, Buffalo Chapter; Alpha Kappa Alpha Sorority, Inc., Gamma Phi Omega Chapter; Women for Human Rights and Dignity; and the American Cancer Society. In 1988, Governor Mario Cuomo appointed her to the Board of Visitors of the

Buffalo Psychiatric Center. She has been re-appointed for a fourth term as a Board of Visitors member.

Several groups have honored her for volunteerism and community activism. She received the *Sojourner Truth Award* from the National Association of Negro Business and Professional Women's Clubs, Inc.; the *Edgar L. Huff Award*, AME Area Missionary Society; Point of Light, New York Conference Branch, Women's Missionary Society; Community Hall of Fame, Bethel Head Start, Community Action Organization (CAO); Golden Heritage Status, NAACP, Buffalo Chapter; *Founders' Day Award*, Alpha Kappa Alpha Sorority, Inc.; and the *Dr. M. Joan Cousin Humanitarian Award*, Ministers Wives, New York Conference Branch.

Ms. Wallace states that her personal philosophy is to be willing to extend a helping hand, whether in the church, social organization, or disciplinary setting, to help find the way without antagonizing.

Uncrowned Queens in the Media

Al-Nisa Banks

For the past twenty years, Al-Nisa Banks has served as editor and publisher of *The Buffalo Challenger*, the largest African American newspaper in the State of New York outside of New York City.

At the age of four she moved to Buffalo with her parents, Billie and the late Eula Banks, who migrated from East Texas, where she was born. The eldest of six children, she grew up in the Black Rock section of the city in the Jasper Parish Housing Projects.

A 1965 graduate of Riverside High School, she received her Bachelor of Arts degree in English from Paine College (a UNCF School) in Augusta, Georgia. Al-Nisa was among the first ten students in the college's history to be named to *Who's Who in American Colleges and Universities*. It also was there that her writing and journalism career began. She served as editor of the college newspaper for two years, and in her senior year, won national competition in the *Reader's Digest* College Essay contest.

Al-Nisa was the second African American to ever hold the position of general assignment reporter for the *Augusta Chronicle* newspaper. She returned to Buffalo in 1971.

Prior to taking the helm at *The Buffalo Challenger*, she worked in various administrative positions and began studies towards her Master's degree at the University at Buffalo. In addition to working as an educator (she headed and developed the curriculum for the first Freedom School in the city in the early seventies), her media experience includes working as an assistant media librarian, television commercial copywriter, news reporter for the *Courier Express*, and editor and co-founder of *Buffalo After Dark* Magazine.

She began her career at *The Buffalo Challenger* as a volunteer in 1979. Today she is part owner and majority stockholder. Al-Nisa is the recipient of nearly one hundred awards and citations both locally and nationally as a result of her work at *The Buffalo Challenger*. In 1980, she was among several black publishers from around the country honored at the United Nations for fair and objective reporting by the

UN's Black American-Arab Friendship Committee. Locally, she was named one of the Citizens of the Year by *The Buffalo News Magazine.*

The subject of numerous feature stories in area publications, Al-Nisa has appeared extensively on local radio and television. Her national exposure includes appearances on Tony Brown's Journal and in *Essence Magazine.* She has traveled widely throughout the United States, West Africa, Haiti, and other parts of the Caribbean.

In addition to constantly striving to improve the scope and quality of *The Buffalo Challenger* and maintain it as a viable business, a relevant institution, and much needed alternative voice for Buffalo's black community, Al-Nisa is an avid student of the healing and internal arts, and hopes to one day be able to further serve humanity through the practice of alternative medicine.

She is the mother of two daughters, Leah and Shola.

Eva M. Doyle

Eva M. Doyle is a columnist, educator, and community activist. She is the author of the column "Eye On History." Her column began in *The Buffalo Challenger* in February 1979 and continues today in the *Buffalo Criterion* – the oldest black newspaper in Western New York. Mrs. Doyle has written thousands of articles on African and African American History during the past twenty-two years. She also is the author of six books. The titles include: *Eye on History, Book 1; Buffalo's Black Community; Motivating Children To Write; Jambo: Let's Count; Celebrating Kwanzaa in Buffalo;* and *Marcus Garvey: Read, Learn and Remember.* Mrs. Doyle also created the *Eye On History Newsletter for Families* and the *Eye On History* series of t-shirts that feature drawings of outstanding African Americans.

As a teacher in the Buffalo Public Schools for the past twenty-six years, her goal has always been to integrate the correct history of African people into the school curriculum. As a result, Mrs. Doyle founded the African American Curriculum Resource Center at the Campus West School in 1994. This Center is the only one of its kind in the entire Buffalo School District. The Center services students, teachers, and the general community by providing a wide array of books, teacher guides, posters, videos, magazines, bibliographies, and general information about the contributions of African people to world civilization.

Mrs. Doyle has been a frequent guest on radio and television programs discussing the issues that surround the African American community, both locally and nationally. She continues to work for the full inclusion of African History into the school curriculum. She serves on a variety of school-based committees such as the Multicultural Educational Instructional Support Team (M.E.I.S.T. Team) and Project S.E.E.D. (Seeking Educational Equity and Diversity). Mrs. Doyle has received over thirty-four awards for her work in the community including the *Woman of Greatness Award*, Life Community Center in Rochester; *Black Achievers in Industry Award*, 1490 Jefferson Enterprises; *Media Award*, Alpha Kappa Alpha Sorority, Inc.; Certificate of Appreciation, Buffalo Board of Education; and Certificate of Appreciation from the Buffalo and Erie County Public Library.

In 1997, Mrs. Doyle was selected as one of thirty-four outstanding teachers nationwide by the American Association of Colleges for Teacher Education to participate in a conference in Washington, D.C. on issues in education.

Mrs. Doyle is married to Romeo Muhammad and is the mother of three and the grandmother of seven children.

Sharon Hanson

Sharon Hanson is Buffalo born and raised. She is the oldest of seven siblings, the mother of two daughters, and grandmother of five: Unique, Darious, Dara, Serina, and Cierra. Her parents are LaRue and the late Marshall L. Hanson.

Currently, she is the Manager of Community Affairs at Adelphia for the Great Lakes Region. Her responsibilities include developing and implementing a variety of programs and projects designed to create a positive and visible image and awareness of

Adelphia throughout the Great Lakes region. Sharon personally represents Adelphia at a variety of public and private sector events, including dinners, receptions, and press conferences. In addition, she accepts and presents awards to and on behalf of Adelphia. She authorizes the production and dissemination of Public Service announcements and promotional product that is delivered across the Cable Television Network. She also participates in the development of a variety of charitable events designed to enhance the image of charitable organizations throughout the community. She hosts a monthly television program designed to bring the community to the television viewer.

Formerly, she was the Special Projects Manager at the Niagara Frontier Transportation Authority, specifically assigned to the Airport Improvement Project. She is proud of her participation with that project, and believes Buffalo now has one of the most outstanding airports in the country.

Ms. Hanson is very active in the community. She serves on the following boards: Vice Chair of the Erie County Medical Center (ECMC), Board of Managers; Executive Vice President of the Board of Directors at the YWCA of Buffalo and Erie County; Trustee on the Board of Trustees at Goodwill Industries; Member of the Erie County Medical Center Lifeline Foundation; and member of the Western New York Housing Development Fund. She also is Associate Co-chair of the Buffalo Region for the United Way 2001 Campaign. She serves on various committees including, The Heritage Centers 50th Anniversary Steering Committee; Chairwoman of the YWCA 2001 Leader Luncheon Awards Program; Springfest 2001 Awards and Dinner Committee; Future of the ECMC Task Force; and several other committees and advisory panels.

She is a graduate of Canisius College, and holds dual Bachelor of Science degrees in English and Political Science. She is a graduate of Leadership Buffalo Class of 1997; a member of the Public Relations Society of America; Cable Television Public Affairs Association; and Women in Cable and Telecommunications; and the Office of Urban Initiatives. She is the recipient of several awards and certificates of honor.

Kawanza McCall

Kawanza McCall is an Account Executive for WGRZ-TV, Channel 2, the local NBC affiliate. Ms. McCall has held several positions in the Engineering, News and Public Relations Departments.

In 1997, Kawanza graduated from the State University of New York at Buffalo, Phi Beta Kappa/Magna Cum Laude, with a dual Bachelor of Arts degree in English and African American Studies. Her college affiliations include: the National Society of Black Engineers (NSBE), Minority Student Recruitment Team, Student Support Services, Minority Academic Achievement Program (MAAP), Collegiate Achievement Program, and Cora P. Maloney College Freshmen Mentor Program. She received scholarships from the Foundation for Minority Interests in Media and the Empire Minority Scholar Program. Kawanza also was inducted into *Who's Who Among Students in American Universities and Colleges*.

An active member of the Western New York community, Ms. McCall belongs to the Buffalo Alumnae Chapter of Delta Sigma Theta Sorority, Inc.; Juneteenth of Buffalo, Inc.; and North Buffalo Junior Athletic Association. In addition, she has worked with the Community Advisory Board for P.S. #36 and P.S. #76, and the Western New York and Finger Lakes Chapter of the Leukemia Society.

A native of Buffalo, she is the daughter of Celestine and the late Rodney McCall, Sr. Ms. McCall is a member of the First Shiloh Baptist Church.

Aviva Merritt

While working evenings as a Nursing Aide in 1958, Aviva attended Nursing School and became a Licensed Practical Nurse, thus beginning her career at Buffalo Children's Hospital. At the time, there were very few skilled African American nurses. She was trained to be a surgical nurse and worked labor and delivery. She later worked in childcare and mental health systems.

In 1977, she began her career as an Account Agent with Allstate Insurance Company. In July 1999, after twenty-two years of service, she retired as the Senior Female Agent in the Buffalo/Rochester region.

During her last two years with Allstate, Aviva served as President of the Board of Directors for the Sickle Cell Disease Association of America (SCDAA), Buffalo, and Western New York Chapter, Inc. She continued to devote time and attention to SCDAA, which had lost funding and its executive director. Aviva assumed the role of Acting Director for one year (without payment) of SCDAA after her retirement, and funding was restored and the office moved to a more suitable location. In February 2000, the Board appointed her Executive Director.

She also is past Board President of Kensington-Bailey Neighborhood Housing Services and continues to serve as Board Secretary. She is past Board member of United Negro College where for five years she raised money with the celebrated "Jammin' Women," and past Board Member of Langston Hughes Institute. She is currently Treasurer of Geneva B. Scruggs Board of Directors.

Aviva currently hosts a cable television show entitled aptly *AVIVA*, which informs, inspires, and entertains. She also is working on a book entitled *AVIVAISMS*, and works as a motivational speaker to young African American females with a program entitled Building SHEROS.

Aviva is the recipient of many community awards including one for Meritorious Community Service for her work with SCDAA from the Buffalo Soldiers, a Washington, D.C.-based group of Buffalonians.

She is a graduate of Leadership Buffalo 2001 and is a *Black Achiever* awardee (2000).

As founder and President of the Nursing Guild of the Evangelistic Temple and Community Church Center, where she is a life-long member, she strives to improve the health of the members of the congregation. The Church was involved in the pilot of *Moving In Faith* which is associated with the Heart and Stroke Association, to combine faith and a healthy lifestyle. She also holds memberships in the NAACP, Buffalo Urban League (and member of the Guild), Afro-American Historical Association of the Niagara Frontier, and officer of the Mary B. Talbert Civic and Cultural Club, which was honored as the first Club inducted into the Uncrowned Queens Web site.

The Arthritis Foundation currently employs Aviva as Program Manager. She resides in Buffalo and is the mother of two, Joyce (Ronald) Walker and Ryan Richards. She also is grandmother of three grandsons, Ronald, Ryan Jr., and Robert.

Uncrowned Queens in Organized Labor

Vastye Gillespie

Vastye W. Gillespie obtained a Bachelor of Arts degree in Public Communications from Buffalo State College. An Arthur A. Schomburg Graduate Fellow, she earned a Juris Doctorate degree from the State University of New York at Buffalo, School of Law and was awarded State and Local Government Law Certification.

As an attorney for the UAW-GM Legal Services Plan since 1995, she represents hundreds of clients per year in consumer issues as well as other legal matters. As a consumer advocate, she provides Pro-Bono legal services to indigent consumers who have been defrauded. Prior to joining the Plan, she practiced in criminal, family, and landlord tenant law.

As a health advocate, Ms. Gillespie serves on the Council of the American Diabetes Association's Cultural Diversity Committee. The committee is responsible for implementing a diabetes awareness campaign targeted at culturally diverse and at-risk populations. She is a Team Captain for the third consecutive year for the Leukemia and Lymphoma Society's Annual *Light the Night Walk*. The walk raises funds to support the Society's mission to cure leukemia, lymphoma, Hodgkin's disease, and mylenoma and to improve the quality of life of patients and their families. She also served as a former board member of Sheehan Memorial Hospital.

Ms. Gillespie is an adjunct professor in the Communication Department of Buffalo State College. She teaches a mass media law course and a diversity course that analyzes how minorities are portrayed in the media.

She serves as Secretary on the Board of Trustees for the Mark Twain Museum of Buffalo.

Ms. Gillespie was one of five panelists at an AFL-CIO working woman symposium with Hillary Clinton in 1999, and is a recipient of *Business First's Forty Under 40* award (1999).

Geraldine Augusta Rolston Mayfield

Geraldine Augusta Rolston was born on May 6, 1919, in Montreal, Canada, to parents Jeri and Marion Emily Clay Rolston. Her family moved to Ft. Erie, Canada, and then to Buffalo, New York, where she became a United States citizen while still an infant. She graduated from Bennett Park School No. 32 in 1934, and from Hutchinson Central High School in 1938.

After working briefly as a teacher aide at a nursery school, Geraldine began working for the United Steel Workers of America (USWA) international union. When she was hired at the union in 1939, she became the first African American member of the secretarial pool in the USWA's office in Lackawanna, New York. During the early 1960s, she became the first African American receptionist at the USWA District 4 central office in Buffalo. In 1972, she was promoted to private secretary to the director of USWA District 4; thus making her the first African American district secretary in the history of the union. Her duties included hiring, training, and coordinating the secretarial staff in district offices throughout New York State, managing the financial operations of all district offices, serving as secretary-treasurer of the district's compensation committee, and maintaining records of union membership. Until she retired in 1983, she was known as "Geri from the Steel Workers" by all of her colleagues and associates in the community.

Geraldine also had a number of interests outside of work. She took several post-high school courses during the 1960s in order to grow professionally as a legal and business secretary. She also studied the German language at the International Institute in Buffalo so that she could effectively communicate with her brother's wife in Buffalo and her in-laws in Germany. After retirement, she joined several bridge clubs, earned Master status in the American Contract Bridge League, and was elected treasurer of the Humboldt Bridge Club. She learned to use a computer to write a number of autobiographical stories and to keep financial records for one of her bridge clubs. She also enjoyed time with her family.

Geraldine's husband was the late Alfonso Mayfield. They had two children, Marion Lela and the late Alfonso Geri Mayfield. She is survived by four grandchildren and five great-grandchildren following her death at the age of eighty on April 20, 2000.

Uncrowned Queens in Politics and Government

Lynn Gilmore Canton

Lynn Gilmore Canton was appointed Executive Director of the Federal Emergency Management Agency (FEMA) during in the administration of President Bill Clinton on June 1, 2000. She was responsible for overseeing the Agency's personnel and management issues, employee development diversity, labor partnership, and strategic planning.

Prior to her appointment to this post, she served as the Agency's Region II Director in New York City. In this position, she was responsible for the administration of Federal emergency preparedness, mitigation, and disaster response and recovery programs for New Jersey, New York, Puerto Rico, and the United States Virgin Islands. Ms. Canton experienced twenty-two natural disasters in Region II during her tenure which included hurricanes, floods, ice and snowstorms, tornadoes, and wild fires. The federal expenditure for disaster relief in the region was over three billion dollars.

In March 2001, Ms. Canton was named the Assistant Deputy Comptroller for Management Audit in the Office of the State Comptroller, H. Carl McCall.

A native of Buffalo and a resident of Clifton Park, New York, Ms. Canton has dedicated her twenty-five year career to public service. Throughout her career she has had extensive experience managing people, programs, and budgets.

Prior to being appointed to the FEMA post, Ms. Canton served as Executive Director of the Division of Minority and Women's Business Development for the Department of Economic Development of New York State. During her tenure in that post, Ms. Canton also served as Chairperson of the New York State Affirmative Action Advisory Council and of the Task Force on the Status of Women in the New York State Department of Economic Development.

Earlier in her career, Ms. Canton served for four years as a member of the New York State Board of Parole. She also worked for the State Division for Youth, the Executive Chamber under the administration of Governor Hugh Carey, and for the Division of the Budget.

Ms. Canton holds Bachelor of Arts and Master of Science degrees from the State University of New York at Albany.

Minnie Gillette

Minnie Gillette was the first African American woman elected to the Erie County Legislature (1977) and had the backing of the Democratic, Republican, and Conservative parties. Shortly after her election into the Legislature, she allied herself with Republican legislators. She was considered a feisty political figure who strayed from party lines in the interest of her constituents.

As a legislator, Ms. Gillette, a former director of the Model Cities Program and past vice president of the Ellicott Community Action Organization, led the movement to convert the former main post office building on Ellicott Street in Buffalo into the Erie Community College City Campus. She also helped establish the Ram Van, a traveling lending library, and fought to help minority contractors receive a fair share of county contracts. She served two terms in the County Legislature, losing re-election in 1981.

Ms. Gillette was appointed as the first director of the county's Victim/Witness Assistance Program, and also served as an election inspector. During this time, she continued to work for a food pantry in the Towne Gardens housing development. Ms. Gillette, coordinator of food distribution to the hungry, received a Martin Luther King award in 1990 at the annual Martin Luther King Awards Dinner sponsored by the Erie County Chapter of the Southern Christian Leadership Conference.

Before becoming involved in politics, she was active in such organizations as the Community Action Organization and the Western New York Health Systems Agency. For many years she worked at Columbus Hospital as dietary supervisor. She obtained her Bachelor of Science degree in nutrition from Buffalo State College.

Ms. Gillette sat on the Board of Managers of the William-Emslie YMCA and helped establish the senior citizens center there. She served as a chairwoman of the Seventh (Ellicott) District Planning Board, and on the Advisory Board of the University at Buffalo's Educational Opportunity Center. She was the President of the New York State Community Action Agency.

She was a past president of the Association for Retarded Children. In 1986, Governor Mario Cuomo appointed her to the Board of Visitors of the West Seneca Developmental Center. She was past Worthy Matron of Paramount Chapter 57 of the Order of the Eastern Star, and also was a member of the advisory board of the Jesse E. Nash Health Center.

As an early member of the Black Leadership Forum, Ms. Gillette organized block clubs and helped register voters throughout her civic career. She was a member of the Erie County Chapter of the Southern Christian Leadership Conference and the Buffalo chapter of the National Association for the Advancement of Colored People. In 1980, she received the University at Buffalo's *Outstanding Women of Western New York Government Award. The Buffalo News* also honored her as Outstanding Citizen for 1979.

Ms. Gillette died on January 7, 1992 at the age of 62.

Beverly A. Gray

Beverly A. Gray was born Beverly A. Rennick in Philadelphia, Pennsylvania in 1950. She is the youngest daughter of William and Bertha Rennick. The family relocated to Buffalo, New York, in 1958. She is the former wife of Mr. Richard D. Gray and the mother of Richard D. Gray, Jr. Ms. Gray grew up and still resides in the Masten District, located on the city's east side.

Ms. Gray, being a small business owner and operator, was elected Councilmember-At-Large for the City of Buffalo in November 1995. She is the first African American woman in the history of Buffalo politics to hold a citywide office. She was sworn in and seated as Councilmember-At-Large on January 1, 1996.

146

In Councilmember Gray's first term as an elected official, she made her mark on the city as being outspoken as it relates to political, economic, and social injustice in the way government delivers services. She was unconventional based on her natural ability to plan, develop, and implement projects. Councilmember Gray established an open door policy in her first year making her the most publicly accessible member in local government, setting her apart from her colleagues.

She was appointed Chair to the Civil Service Committee; member of the Education, Finance, Police Reorganization and Oversight Subcommittee; in addition to chairing a special committee on Taxicab reform. Ms. Gray initiated revising the CURA plan for the city's east side, emphasizing economic redevelopment of commercial strips within inner city neighborhoods, in conjunction with preservation initiatives of existing commercial strips. The once commercially vibrant Jefferson Avenue is the current focus of her economic re-development plans. Ms. Gray secured 3.5 million dollars to design and construct a state-of-the-art Telecommunication Center as an anchor tenant for Jefferson Avenue. The historic Apollo Theater property now houses The Buffalo Municipal Communications Center, Public Education and Government (PEG channels).

Ms. Gray won re-election in 1999. As an At-Large member, she attends all committee meetings, enabling her to be well informed on City of Buffalo issues affecting the voter and tax base. She has held several positions as chair and committee-member during her tenure on the Council. She was appointed Chair of the Community Development Committee that oversees the distribution of the Federal Block Grant entitlement program with the Federal under the guidelines of the Department of Housing and Urban Development (HUD).

In 2000, Ms. Gray was elected to the State Democratic Judicial Committee. She was the first woman to run for Mayor in Buffalo's history, and the first in opposition to an incumbent Mayor in 2001.

Her humanitarian activities are extensive. She works with community groups and block clubs from across the city. She initiated the dialogue that led to the building of the 6th Precinct in the forgotten African American community.

She is a member of many social, civil, and political groups including the NAACP; Buffalo Urban League, local chapter; United

Negro College Fund; WNED public television; Greater East Side Business Association; Family Day Care Association, local chapter; Black Chamber of Commerce; Women for Human Rights and Dignity (WHRD); and the Women's Pavilion Pan American 2001. She is former First Vice President of Grassroots, Inc.; current Board Member of the Community Action Organization of Erie County; former Board Member of Minority Coalition, Inc.; and a volunteer for Project Joy.

Ms. Gray is a member of the Metropolitan United Methodist Church. She participated in the re-enactment of the Slave Crossing of the Niagara River to Freedom that is sponsored annually by the Buffalo Quarters Historical Society. She is Chaplain of the Harriet Tubman 300s; a group whose mandate is to mark historical sites used by runaway slaves.

Renae Kimble

Niagara County Legislator Renae Kimble was elected November 2, 1993, representing the Second Legislative District in the city of Niagara Falls and was re-elected to her fourth two-year term on November 2, 1999. In 1991, Ms. Kimble was the first woman to run for Mayor of the City of Niagara Falls.

She graduated from Niagara County Community College with an Associate in Arts degree and the State University of New York at Buffalo with a Bachelor of Arts degree in Political Science. She also holds a Faculty of Law and Jurisprudence with a Juris Doctor Degree from the University at Buffalo.

Legislator Kimble has been a strong voice and advocate for the residents of her district, as well as the residents of Niagara County. She is not afraid to take on the tough issues and has a reputation as a tough, but fair, no-nonsense legislator. She has accrued more name recognition and notoriety than any other Niagara County Legislator.

In her freshman year of office, Legislator Kimble was the sponsor of the grant application to the United States Department of Housing and Urban Development, Micro Enterprise Program. As a result, the County received a $600,000 grant to provide technical assistance and capital, with the goal of creating viable and productive small businesses in Niagara County. In 1996, the County was awarded an additional 1.8 million dollars for this program, for a total of 2.4 million dollars. Over 190 small businesses have benefited from the technical assistance provided by the Micro Enterprise program. Sixty percent of the program's participants have been women and minorities. As a member of the Micro Enterprise Assistance Program Loan Review panel, Legislator Kimble has been responsible for awarding approximately $650,000 in low interest loans to small businesses in Niagara County.

As the former Chairwoman of the Administration Committee, she was instrumental in promoting and developing a local law establishing a County Code of Ethics. The law was unanimously passed on February 19, 1996, and took effect on April 1, 1996. The Code of Ethics established minimum standards of appropriate conduct for County officials and employees, as well as members of advisory boards, committees, or commissions. This Code is considered the toughest Code of Ethics in the State of New York.

As a former member of the Finance Committee, Legislator Kimble worked diligently to produce a three-year, zero percent tax increase and a two million dollar reduction the fourth year. An effective lawmaker, Legislator Kimble is a former Majority Leader of the Niagara County Legislature, the only African American to hold this position. She is the first and only African American woman to be elected to public office in the County of Niagara.

Accomplishments of Legislator Kimble include, but are not limited to: securing a $25,000 grant for the Niagara Community Center to purchase a van and computer; reopening of the 13th Street Gym after it closed in 1997; proposing legislation for the Niagara County takeover of the Niagara Falls Airport; restoring bus service after the Niagara Frontier Transit Authority proposed cuts; providing two 500 dollar NOVA Scholarships to the Niagara County Black Achievers Committee in 1999 and 2000; serving as the General Chairperson for the 25th Annual Black Achievers Scholarship Awards Banquet; legislating the County's Red, Yellow, Green Smoking Sign Ordinance that promotes choice and freedom for both smokers and non-smokers.

A former Director of the Niagara Falls Human Rights Commission - the first woman to hold this position - she is an advocate for the rights of all people, and is a strong voice for change.

Her strong faith in God and acceptance of her Lord and Savior Jesus Christ is her greatest source of strength, which enables her to serve each and every resident of Niagara County with tremendous zeal and humility. Legislator Kimble is the daughter of Theodis and Lillie Kimble.

Cora P. Maloney

Cora P. Maloney was born in Kansas City, Missouri, and was a graduate of the University of Kansas. She was active in Kansas Democratic politics before moving to Buffalo.

In 1957, she was sworn in as a committeewoman in the Sixth District of the 13th ward. She was Buffalo's first councilwoman, the first Democrat ever to be elected in the Masten District, and the first African American to be elected in the district in twenty years.

Mrs. Maloney was president of Buffalo Intro-Club Council for two years as well as president of the Democratic Business and Professional Women's Club. She was active in the Niagara Buffalo Links and the Fitness Study Club. In addition, she was past chairwoman of the Buffalo Urban League Guild, a member of the Niagara Frontier Association of Medical Technologists, the Masten District Youth Board, Emma V. Kelly Temple 700.1BFOEW, Alpha Kappa Alpha Scholastic Sorority, and the Women's Committee of the New York State Fair.

The Democratic Business and Professional Women's Club, founded by Mrs. Maloney, established a Cora P. Maloney Scholarship Fund, which is awarded each year to a young woman studying in the field of Medical Arts, pharmacy, nursing, or medical technology. The Cora P. Maloney College at the University at Buffalo is named in her honor.

She was married to the former Assistant Attorney General, Clarence M. Maloney.

Cora P. Maloney died on August 16, 1961. She is interred at Forest Lawn Cemetery in Buffalo.

Lillian Meadows

Lillian Meadows, supervisor of the Alfred D. Price Senior Citizens Center in the Buffalo Municipal Hosing Authority (formerly the Willert Park project), became the second African American woman to serve on the Old Erie County Board of Supervisors from 1965-68. She was preceded by Pauline McGowan.

Mrs. Meadows also was the first African American to win a city-wide primary election here in 1961 when she ran for councilwoman-at-large. She was defeated by a close margin in the general election. In addition, she was the first black woman to serve as state committee-woman in this area that same year.

Crystal D. Peoples

Crystal D. Peoples has served the community as 7th District Erie County Legislator since 1993. Her dedication to an agenda that seeks social, economic, educational, environmental, and legal justice remains unparalleled in the political arena.

She was born, raised, and educated in Buffalo. She is a homeowner, mother, grandmother, and activist who has demonstrated remarkable dedication to God, family, community, and country throughout her professional career. Her work has enhanced the quality of life in the 7th District as well as all of Western New York. In addition to her duties as an elected official, Legislator Peoples served as Majority Leader and Chairperson of the Erie County Legislature's Finance Committee, which oversees an annual budget of one billion dollars, for five of the eight years she has been a member of the Erie County Legislature.

Legislator Peoples is the recipient of hundreds of awards and salutations. She supports little league sports, libraries, and neighborhood beautification and clean up projects. She encourages block clubs to empower themselves by organizing and working closely together. Ms. Peoples holds public hearings and forums on issues relevant to her community such as crack/cocaine usage, business development, HIV/AIDS, and regionalism. Her district office has served hundreds of Western New York residents, linking them with service providers and advocating for their rights to access services and information. She has sponsored public education campaigns that address social ills, housing, and economic development, and funded educational initiatives such as Fight the Blight; HIV/AIDS Peer Education; and the Respect Yourself, Respect Your World anti-litter and graffiti campaign. She commissioned a Blue Ribbon Committee to study the connection between poor housing and preventative health conditions and the prospect of setting countywide minimum housing standards. Legislator Peoples is the author of the MBE/WBE law and certification program which generates millions of dollars in annual revenue to minority and women owned businesses in Erie County by giving them access to government purchasing and service contracts. She successfully lobbied state government to change real property tax laws and sponsored legislation that allows Erie County residents to make partial payments on back taxes. It was Legislator Peoples efforts that drove collaboration between all levels of government and brought the Jefferson Avenue Tops Market economic development initiative to fruition. Legislator Peoples flew to Washington, D.C., and personally requested the assistance of United States Senator Chuck Schumer to bring closure to an economic development project that will give 113,000 inner-city residents direct access to fresh fruits and vegetables, create jobs, and increase surrounding property values. The current focus of her legislative efforts is economic development, cultural tourism and heritage, maintaining Western New York's only public hospital, and generating wealth in her community.

Legislator Peoples' motto is, "the quality of your life is the purpose of my politics." Her leadership illustrates that she not only talks the talk, but walks the walk and her commitment to family and community cannot be duplicated, diminished, nor denied.

Yvonne Scruggs-Leftwich

Dr. Yvonne Scruggs-Leftwich is an author, public scholar, policy analyst, community activist, and spokesperson on behalf of creative black leadership and urban politics.

As executive director and chief operating officer of the Black Leadership Forum, Inc., a twenty-three year confederation of the top national civil rights and service organizations, she facilitates dialogue among African American leadership and designs opportunities for collaboration, across racial lines, on issues important to the community. She also is a professor of Urban Power Politics at several nationally recognized universities.

Dr. Scruggs-Leftwich received a Ph.D. from the University of Pennsylvania, a Master's degree from the Hubert H. Humphrey School of the University of Minnesota, and a Bachelor's degree from North Carolina Central University. She also was a Fulbright Fellow to Germany.

Previously she was deputy Mayor of Philadelphia; New York State's Housing Commissioner; HUD's Deputy Assistant Secretary; Executive Director of President Carter's Urban and Regional Policy Group which issued the first formal National Urban Policy over two decades ago; and director of the Urban and National Policy Institutes for the Joint Center for Political and Economic Studies in Washington. Dr. Scruggs-Leftwich co-owned several non-depository banking corporations and has served as a consulting vice president in the municipal finance field.

She is regularly quoted in newspapers around the country and has been profiled in *The New York Times*, *The Washington Post* and other publications. She is a commentator on the *News Hour with Jim Lehrer* and appears frequently on many other public affairs broadcast shows.

Dr. Scruggs-Leftwich has written over one hundred publications. She writes a syndicated column for The National Newspaper Association and is working on her next book, *Sound Bites of Protest: Race, Politics and Public Policy*.

She has been a professor at several top universities throughout her career including Howard University and the University of Pennsylvania. She is listed in *Who's Who Among Black Americans; Who's Who in America; Who's Who Among American Women;* and her career and life are described in the *Biography of African American Women.*

Her areas of expertise include urban policy, public administration and governmental behavior, black women as activists and change agents, city and regional planning, developing neighborhoods and small communities, strategic planning, and leadership development.

She is the daughter of Uncrowned Queen, Geneva B. Scruggs.

Uncrowned Queens in Religion

Jacqueline A. Foye

Jacqueline Foye was born in Goldsboro, North Carolina. After losing her mother at a very early age, Jacqueline was reared, along with six sisters and one brother, in an Apostolic home by her father, Deacon Monroe Bryant. She attended the School Street Elementary School and Dillard High School, of which she graduated in 1953.

In 1955, she married her high-school sweetheart James E. Foye, Sr. They had three children, James, Jr., Valerie, and Tracey. She also is grandmother to James, III, Jasmine, and Christian.

Following a business career in New York City, she continued her education at Erie Community College (ECC) in Buffalo. She was employed for four years by the Buffalo Board of Education, after which she worked for the Health Department and as a manager for Liberty Shoe Store.

Through the years she has worked in the church, organizing choirs in various cities and states along the east coast. For twenty-five years she worked faithfully as the Minister of Music for Emmanuel Temple Church in Buffalo under the leadership of the late Bishop William Crossley. Her service was not in the church alone, but also in the community. She volunteered her time to tutoring remedial reading, making home and hospital visitations, also working with the Community Action Organization (CAO) programs, and the PTA.

In 1979, she was appointed pastor and overseer of the Apostolic House of Prayer (AHOP). The former building of AHOP was gutted and reconstructed by Deacon James E. Foye, Sr., and a new edifice was completed in 1993. Pastor Jacqueline Foye was honored as the First African American Woman to build a church in the State of New York. There are many more visions and goals for AHOP, such as a Community Outreach Program to assist the homeless and those in need, a daycare, school, and housing facility.

The most challenging experience in Foye's life was when she attended the Seminary of Religious Justice. During her study at the seminary she embraced a new perspective toward pastoral care and counseling. She graduated in 1999.

Through the years, Pastor Foye has labored in God's vineyard, and with grace and help from above she will continue to work until the day is done. It is her firm belief that God has given her, "faith that conquers anything."

Velma Jones

Velma Jones was born and educated in Roxboro, North Carolina. She later relocated to Buffalo where she met and married Bishop Leroy Jones. She is the mother of seven children and grandmother to six.

Having received Christ more than thirty years ago, Evangelist Jones subsequently acknowledged her call to the ministry. Now, as an ordained minister of the gospel, she serves on the pastoral staff of the Cold Spring Church of God in Christ where her late husband formerly served as pastor.

God has blessed her ministry greatly by opening doors and allowing her to exercise her gift all over the United States. In her extensive travels, Evangelist Jones has ministered on several occasions at the Potters House of Dallas, Texas, and has taught and preached at numerous women conferences, retreats, and special services.

Desiring to become all that she can be in Christ has set Evangelist Jones upon a course of study with the Rhema Bible School from which she will receive a degree in Bible studies.

Her heartfelt desire is to be instrumental in seeing the body of Christ grow in a first-love relationship with the Father and to walk in the ministry of reconciliation. Sister Jones' ministry of reconciliation has truly been anointed and blessed by God.

Noma L. Roberson

*The tongue that brings forth healing
is a tree of life.*
Proverbs 15:4

Before the foundation of the world, God ordained the life, ministry, and work of His vessel of healing, Dr. Noma L. Roberson. Faced with some of the same challenges as the prophets of old, God anointed Dr. Roberson to combat many of the spiritual, mental, and physical sicknesses that plague the world today. Through her steadfast relationship with Him, God has entrusted her with the mandate to minister healing and deliverance through evangelism and medical research throughout the world.

Handcrafted by the potter for such a time as this, Dr. Roberson currently serves as an Evangelist and District Missionary in the Western New York Jurisdiction #2 of the Church of God in Christ, under the leadership of Bishop Glennwood H. Young, Sr., and Supervisor Margaret Woods. She attends Saints' Home Church of God in Christ, where her pastor is Bishop Carl Roberson. With membership totaling thirty-nine years in the Church of God in Christ and thirty-two years at her present church, Dr. Roberson has served her local church faithfully.

Seeking to acclimate every believer to the place, power, and sufficiency of the cross of Jesus, Dr. Roberson has served in several positions in the local, jurisdictional, and national church. She served as a Workshop Instructor (Health Measures) in the International Women's Department of the Church of God in Christ, District Secretary of the Women's Department, District and Local President of Pastors' and Ministers' Wives, President of the Saints' Home Department of Women, and teacher of Bible Study. In addition, God has anointed Dr. Roberson to conduct church services, seminars, retreats, and conferences across the nation.

Dr. Roberson has illustrated the glory of God through numerous educational accomplishments. She completed a Master of Science degree in Natural Science in 1978, and a doctorate in Experimental

Pathology-Epidemiology and Cancer Control in 1985, at the State University of New York at Buffalo, School of Medicine and Biomedical Sciences.

Currently, Dr. Roberson is the President and Chief Executive Officer of Roberson Consulting International, headquartered in Amherst, New York. Prior to this position, Dr. Roberson had a twenty-nine-year tenure at Roswell Park Cancer Institute in Buffalo. As an epidemiologist and cancer control specialist at this Institute, Dr. Roberson was Director of Community Intervention Research. One of her national achievements as director was the design and operation of a 34-foot mobile health and screening van.

Dr. Roberson has published numerous articles from her research and is the author of three books. She is a member of numerous international, national, regional, and local professional boards and committees. In addition, she is the recipient of more than thirty awards of achievement.

As Dr. Roberson continues to fulfill the work of Christ, she gives God the glory for her husband of thirty-two years, Elder Willie C. Roberson, two daughters, Cheronn Roberson and Sundra Ryce, son-in-law, Stephen Ryce, and two grandsons, Jonathan and Joshua.

Josephine H. Thompson

Josephine H. Thompson was the sixth of eleven children born to Mr. and Mrs. Arthur L. Hunley of Deatsville, Alabama.

She accepted Christ as her savior and joined the St. James Missionary Baptist Church where she was later baptized in Mortar Creek. As a child she was inspired by the Word and would go to a stump near her home to pray, never realizing God's program was in progress – *From the stump to the pulpit*.

Josephine was an active member of her church and worked in all the auxiliaries. Along with her late husband, she organized a family singing group. The group sang throughout the cities of Buffalo, Cleveland, Erie, Niagara Falls, Youngstown, and Baltimore.

She loved being on the Usher Board, doing missionary work, and singing in the choir. But that was not all that God had in store for her. There was a turning point in her life. Being born in Jesus, she was called to the ministry in 1957. Due to the Orthodox Baptist rulings concerning Women Ministers, she separated from Calvary and united with the St. Paul's Missionary Baptist Church and was licensed by the Reverend M. Tidwell. In the same year Reverend Thompson became the Assistant Pastor. She held that post faithfully until 1959, at which time she became Pastor of St. Paul's.

During a journey to the desert of Arizona, Reverend Thompson was inspired to organize African-American women into the ministry according to their divine calling. In 1958, she formed the Women Ministers' Christian Association and established chapters in Baltimore, Detroit, Buffalo, and Cleveland. She has been a national leader and primary advocate for the ordination of black women into the ministry of Jesus Christ in America. She also has been one of the powerful forces in the field of religion to empower and strengthen the role of black women in the leadership of church and society.

She continues to help and aid all people who are called to do God's work and accepts the toils and tribulations that man has placed on the shoulders of a woman preaching the Word of God...*Let the works she's done speak for her!*

Shirley Wright-Watts

Born in Chicago, Illinois, Shirley M. Wright-Watts has been a Buffalonian since her youth. The mother of seven, and grandmother of eleven, Shirley has a history of community activity dating back to the 1950s. She began her involvement in the Buffalo Public School system, serving several years as PTA President and Parent Coordinator. She was a strong advocate for quality education and parent involvement in inner city schools and was instrumental in the process to desegregate public schools. For three years she chaired the Education Committee of Citizens' Council On Human Relations, working to bring about improvements in all public schools. She was selected by

Governor Nelson Rockefeller and Buffalo Mayor Frank Sedita to serve on a statewide Council on Public School Issues. Shirley was one of the first teachers in St. Augustine Center's Early Childhood Development Program, and developed the Center's first after-school remedial and enrichment program for elementary grade students.

She worked fifteen years at Buffalo General Hospital Community Mental Health Center, holding positions as counselor, therapist, treatment planner, and became the first female Coordinator of Psychiatric Day Treatment Services. She implemented staff in-service training on Cross Cultural Counseling Concepts in Treatment Modalities, and advocated for Christian Counseling for patients who desired that approach.

Sensing a call to ministry, Shirley retired early in 1989 to begin study for the mission field under the auspices of the Episcopal Church. She became the first African American female sent into foreign mission from the Diocese of Western New York. She was called to the Episcopal Diocese of the Republic of Panama where she worked as counselor, teacher, director of staff development, and grant writer at a residential home for orphaned and abandoned children from impoverished backgrounds. Upon completion of her Panama assignment, she worked as mission consultant/trainer for National Episcopal Church in New York City. She worked with Trinity Baptist Church in Buffalo to finalize plans for the Home Space Project and with other parish-based ministries in the city. Shirley was a co-founder of the Racial/Ethnic Minority Mission Program, under National Church endorsement, designed to promote mission involvement and support for people of color. Under this program, more than eighty-five persons of color have experienced the opportunity to serve as short-term missionaries around the world.

Shirley continues to serve the national church as mission trainer, speaker, Church School curriculum consultant, and sits on international and ecumenical mission boards. She is active at both the Diocesan and parish levels in Buffalo and is a Lay Liturgical Leader at St. Paul's Cathedral. She chairs the Diocesan World Mission Committee and is a member of the Anti-Racism Committee, Hunger Task Force, Companion Diocese Committee, Cathedral Grants Committee, and several other social ministry committees. In 1998, Bishop David Bowman and Cathedral Dean, Allen Farabee, installed Shirley as the first African American Lay Canon in the Diocese at St.

Paul's Cathedral. She is the Canon for Mission and Outreach, advocating for persons in need.

She traveled to South Africa in the fall of 2000, representing the Diocese of Western New York, for the celebration of the tenth anniversary of the Anglican Diocese of Klerksdorp and for the commemoration of the birthplace of Archbishop Desmond Tutu. While in South Africa, she was invited to become a member of the Mother's Union, and was inducted at a special ceremony conducted by South African Bishop and Mrs. David Nkwe in the Bishop's Chapel. Shirley is one of only three African American women admitted to a South African Mother's Union Chapter.

She is committed to her work on behalf of the poor, homeless, hungry, unemployed, refugees from areas of conflict, and others in need. Having traveled to many other countries, she is a witness to social problems from a global perspective. According to Shirley, "No one nation has a monopoly on human suffering and human needs and this reality prompts one to rethink the question of being our brother's (sister's) keepers. My work is in thanksgiving for the faith and fortitude of our ancestors, for the accomplishments of my children, and for all blessings that God has given to us."

Uncrowned Queens in Science

Mamie Beale Johnson

Mamie Beale Johnson is a native of Buffalo. She attended Buffalo P.S. #32 and Hutchinson Central High School. Mrs. Johnson, a graduate of Virginia Union University in Richmond, Virginia, received a Bachelor of Science degree in Mathematics in 1947. Upon returning to Buffalo, Mrs. Johnson, when applying for a job in her field, was considered an "oddity" – a female, a black and a mathematician. After many unsuccessful interviews at agencies, she was eventually hired at Cornell Aeronautical Laboratory in 1948. She served, with distinction, in this position for twenty-two years. She was one of several scientists who were featured in *Ebony Magazine* in 1950.

In 1970, Mrs. Johnson embarked on a new career. She began working at the State University of New York at Buffalo's Educational Opportunity Center. She held several positions during her tenure with EOC. She was the Registrar (1970-1974), Research Assistant (1974-1976), and Community Relations and Recruitment Coordinator from 1977 until 1990 when she retired.

Mrs. Johnson has been involved in community service for over fifty years. She was a charter member of the Buffalo Chapter of Jack and Jill of America, Inc. and also of the Harriet Tubman 300s. In addition, she has been a role model for young people; encouraging many youngsters to enroll in college and volunteering her services as a math tutor for students.

Mrs. Johnson has been a board member of several organizations: Everywoman Opportunity Center, Niagara Frontier Vocational Rehabilitation Center, the United Negro College Fund (UNCF), Ujima Theater Company, the Buffalo Philharmonic Orchestra Women's Committee, and WGRZ-TV2 Minority Advisory Council. She is a member of the Buffalo Chapter of The Links, Incorporated, the Harriet Tubman 300s, and Alpha Kappa Alpha Sorority, Inc.

Some awards and recognitions that she has received include the UNCF *Frederick D. Patterson Distinguished Leadership Award* (1990) and *Meritorious Service Award* (1995), recognition of volunteerism from the Community Action Organization (CAO) Education Task Force (1984-

1994), and recognition for volunteerism from the UNCF (1995-1996 campaign).

Active in church life, she was the former organist for Lloyd's Memorial United Church of Christ for twenty years. Currently, she is a member of Lincoln Memorial United Methodist Church where she participates in Senior Choir and the Emma J. Horner Chorale. She also has served as a church pianist and editor of the church newsletter.

Mrs. Johnson was married to the late Horace "Billy" Johnson. She has three daughters: June Johnson Stanford of Buffalo, Patricia Johnson Isaac of Poughkeepsie, New York, and Holly Johnson Fisher of Atlanta, Georgia. She also has six granddaughters.

About the Authors

Dr. Peggy Brooks-Bertram is a native of Baltimore, Maryland. She received her first doctorate from The Johns Hopkins University School of Hygiene and Public Health. She received a second doctorate in American Studies at the State University of New York at Buffalo. Dr. Bertram is the founder and CEO of Jehudi Educational Services, an independent consulting firm specializing in K-12 curriculum development, staff development, training, and conference and seminar planning. She is a specialist in grant writing and proposal development in health care, history, education, and environmental health.

Dr. Bertram is an independent scholar in African American women's history, and is a well-known lecturer and only known authority on the life and writings of Drusilla Dunjee Houston. She authored numerous editorials from 1989-1995 on the Buffalo Board of Education and other topics for *The Buffalo Challenger* newspaper. In addition, she is Adjunct Assistant Professor at the University at Buffalo.

She has authored several book chapters in health, specifically depression, including "Social and Psychological Aspects of Women's Health: A Diversified Perspective" in *Psychiatric Issues in Women* (U. Halbreich, Editor, 1997); and "African American Women: Disfigured Images in the Epidemiology of Depression" in *African American Women and Health* (Catherine F. Collins, Editor, 1997). Her publications on ancient African history include "The Sixth Napatan Dynasty of Kush," in *Journal of African Civilizations* (1994). She also is the author of five unpublished children's books in the *Africa on My Stairs* series and numerous other poems and essays on ancient Africa.

A native of Louisiana, Dr. Barbara A. Seals Nevergold moved to Buffalo, New York with her family in 1947. She completed a Bachelor of Science degree in French Education at the State University College at Buffalo and has two Master's degrees; one in French Education and one in Counseling Education from the University at Buffalo. In addition, she earned a Doctor of Philosophy degree at UB in Counseling Education. She has studied in Quebec, Canada at Laval University and in France at the University of Dijon.

She has been employed by several organizations that have served the interests of women, children, and families. Currently, she is the Director of Student Support Services at the University at Buffalo's Educational Opportunity Center. She also is an instructor at Empire State College where she teaches courses in Domestic Violence, Counseling, Marriage and Family, Human Sexuality, Cultural Diversity, Child Welfare, and Human Service Delivery Systems.

Dr. Nevergold has authored several published articles including "Fantastic Color and Special Effects: The Seals Ebony Studio" in the Spring 2002 edition of *Western New York Heritage Magazine*; "To Be an Instrument for Their Voices: Finding, Writing, and Sharing Family Histories in Afro-Americans" in *New York Life and History* (Volume 25, Number 2, July 2001); and "Transracial Adoption: In the Child's Best Interest?" in *African American Women's Health and Social Issues*, Catherine F. Collins, Editor.

Individually, Drs. Bertram and Nevergold have received numerous community service and educational awards. Their joint honors for the Uncrowned Queens Project include the *William Wells Brown Award* from the Afro-American Historical Association of the Niagara Frontier for their efforts to chronicle and preserve local African American history. The University at Buffalo honored them with both the *UB Star Award* (2001) for outstanding work on the Pan-American Exposition Centennial celebration and the *Service Excellence Award* (2002) in recognition of their work to "advance the basic mission of University Services." Drs. Bertram and Nevergold also are the recipients of the *Excellence in Education Award* from Xi Epsilon Omega Chapter of Alpha Kappa Alpha Sorority, Inc.; the *President's Award for Community Service* from the Mary B. Talbert Civic and Cultural Club; and the *2002 Community Service Award* from the Buffalo Urban League. Further, the Uncrowned Queens Project was honored by the City of Buffalo and Erie County Legislature with proclamations declaring February 15, 2001, as *Uncrowned Queens Day*.

Drs. Nevergold and Bertram have co-authored *African, Darkies and Negroes: Black Faces at the Pan American Exposition of 1901* (in press), a book on the history of African and African American involvement in the Pan American Exposition of 1901. Their goal with the Uncrowned Queens Project is to export the model nation-wide to build a network of Uncrowned Queens.

Index